EVENTS THAT
CHANGED THE
WORLD

D0901204

1900–1920

=== The Twentieth Century ===

Other books in the
That Changed the World series:

EVENTS THAT
CHANGED THE
WORLD

1900–1920

═ The Twentieth Century ═

Gary Zacharias, *Book Editor*

Daniel Leone, *President*
Bonnie Szumski, *Publisher*
Scott Barbour, *Managing Editor*

GREENHAVEN
PRESS ®

THOMSON
—✦—™
GALE

San Diego • Detroit • New York • San Francisco • Cleveland
New Haven, Conn. • Waterville, Maine • London • Munich

Cover credit: © Hulton/Archive by Getty Images
Library of Congress, 45, 62
NASA, 52
National Archives, 16, 166, 198

LIBRARY OF CONGRESS CATALOGING-IN-PUBLICATION DATA

1900–1920 / Gary Zacharias, book editor.
p. cm. — (Events that changed the world)
Includes bibliographical references and index.
ISBN 0-7377-1753-X (pbk. : alk. paper) — ISBN 0-7377-1752-1 (lib. : alk. paper)
1. World politics—1900–1918. 2. World War, 1914–1918—Causes. 3. Sea power—History—20th century. 4. Technological innovations. 5. Inventions. 6. World War, 1939–1945—Causes. I. Zacharias, Gary. II. Series.
D421.A1232 2004
909.82'1—dc21   2003048332

Printed in the United States of America

CONTENTS

Event 3: Theodore Roosevelt Becomes President: September 14, 1901

Event 4: The Wright Brothers Fly the First Heavier-than-Air Craft: December 17, 1903

out one special painting that changed how art could be used for more than depicting the real world.

Event 9: Ernest Rutherford Discovers the Structure of the Atomic Nucleus: 1911

Event 10: The *Titanic* Sinks: April 14, 1912

in mass media, better maritime regulations, and the creation of a powerful myth that still reverberates today.

Event 11: The Assassination of the Archduke Ferdinand: June 28, 1914

1. An Assassination Drags Europe into War

The assassination of an Austro-Hungarian archduke at the hand of a Serbian nationalist led a large number of European nations into the most savage warfare the world had ever seen.

Event 12: The Battle of the Marne Produces Stalemate in World War I: September 6–10, 1914

1. The Allies Stop the German Onslaught

The Germans had a great opportunity to end the war quickly in 1914, but Allied resistance and German blunders caused the two sides to turn the fighting into static trench warfare.

Event 13: The Release of *The Birth of a Nation:* 1915

1. *The Birth of a Nation* Becomes the First Blockbuster

Movies became a big part of the entertainment industry thanks to a few early pioneers, including D.W. Griffith. *The Birth of a Nation*, with its controversial theme and innovative cinematic techniques, became the first huge movie success.

lization was optimistic about the future and proud of its accomplishments. But after four terrible years of fighting, the optimism and pride turned to despair. The Western world questioned its basic values.

Event 18: The Treaty of Versailles: June 28, 1919

1. The Treaty of Versailles Is Signed

Four years of slaughter left both sides exhausted in 1918. The Allied leaders determined to make Germany pay dearly for the ordeal.

2. Aftermath of the Treaty: The League of Nations Provides a Model for Global Cooperation

Today people often ridicule the League of Nations for its failure to stop the aggression of Hitler and Mussolini in the 1930s. But the league, a direct result of the Treaty of Versailles, had some successes and held out hope for a better, more peaceful world.

FOREWORD

In 1543 a Polish astronomer named Nicolaus Copernicus published a book entitled *De revolutionibus orbium coelestium* in which he theorized that Earth revolved around the Sun. In 1688, during the Glorious Revolution, Dutch prince William of Orange invaded England and overthrew King James II. In 1922 Irish author James Joyce's novel *Ulysses*, which describes one day in Dublin, was published.

Although these events are seemingly unrelated, occurring in different nations and in different centuries, they all share the distinction of having changed the world. Although Copernicus's book had a relatively minor impact at the time of its publication, it eventually had a momentous influence. The Copernican system provided a foundation on which future scientists could develop an accurate understanding of the solar system. Perhaps more importantly, it required humanity to contemplate the possibility that Earth, far from occupying a special place at the center of creation, was merely one planet in a vast universe. In doing so, it forced a reevaluation of the Christian cosmology that had served as the foundation of Western culture. As professor Thomas S. Kuhn writes, "The drama of Christian life and the morality that had been made dependent upon it would not readily adapt to a universe in which the earth was just one of a number of planets."

Like the Copernican revolution, the Glorious Revolution of 1688–1689 had a profound influence on the future of Western societies. By deposing James II, William and his wife, Mary, ended the Stuart dynasty, a series of monarchs who had favored the Catholic Church and had limited the power of Parliament for decades. Under William and Mary, Parliament passed the Bill of Rights, which established the legislative supremacy of Parliament and barred Roman Catholics from the throne. These actions initiated the gradual process by which the power of the government of England shifted from the monarchy to Parliament, establishing a democratic system that would be copied, with some variations, by the United States and other democratic societies worldwide.

Whereas the Glorious Revolution had a major impact in the political sphere, the publication of Joyce's novel *Ulysses* represented a revolution in literature. In an effort to capture the sense of chaos and discontinuity that permeated the culture in the wake of World War I, Joyce did away with the use of straightforward narrative that had dominated fiction up to that time. The novel, whose structure mirrors that of Homer's *Odyssey*, combines realistic descriptions of events with passages that convey the characters' inner experience by means of a technique known as stream of consciousness, in which the characters' thoughts and feelings are presented without regard to logic or narrative order. Due to its departure from the traditional modes of fiction, *Ulysses* is often described as one of the seminal works of modernist literature. As stated by Pennsylvania State University professor Michael H. Begnal, "*Ulysses* is the novel that changed the direction of 20th-century fiction written in English."

Copernicus's theory of a sun-centered solar system, the Glorious Revolution, and James Joyce's *Ulysses* are just three examples of time-bound events that have had far-reaching effects—for better or worse—on the progress of human societies worldwide. History is made up of an inexhaustible list of such events. In the twentieth century alone, for example, one can isolate any number of world-shattering moments: the first performance of Igor Stravinsky's ballet *The Rites of Spring* in 1913; Japan's attack on Pearl Harbor on December 7, 1941; the launch of the satellite *Sputnik* on October 4, 1957. These events variously influenced the culture, society, and political configuration of the twentieth century.

Greenhaven Press's Events That Changed the World series is designed to help readers learn about world history by examining seemingly random events that have had the greatest influence on the development of cultures, societies, and governments throughout the ages. The series is divided into sets of several anthologies, with each set covering a period of one hundred years. Each volume begins with an introduction that provides essential context on the time period being covered. Then, the major events of the era are covered by means of primary and secondary sources. Primary sources include firsthand accounts, speeches, correspondence, and other materials that bring history alive. Secondary sources analyze the profound effects the events had on the world. Each reading is preceded by an introduction that puts it in context and emphasizes the event's importance in the ongoing evolution of world history. Additional features add to the value of the series: An annotated table of contents and an index allow readers to quickly locate material of interest. A chronology provides an easy reference for contextual information. And a bibliography offers opportunities for further exploration. All of these features help to make the Events That Changed the World series a valuable resource for readers interested in the major events that have shaped the course of humanity.

INTRODUCTION

Twenty years is not a long time in world history, but in the twentieth century every twenty-year period encompassed major historical change. The years 1900–1920 involved significant political change: In that short span national and international politics led to a new world order and altered the course of twentieth-century history.

One key event, World War I, was responsible for much of this political change. Warfare is a common thread throughout human history, but no previous war changed the political fortunes of so many nations as did the world conflict that raged from 1914 to 1918. As would be true of World War II, this first international conflict humbled former powers and created new ones. In addition, World War I ended with a peace treaty that would have tremendous political reverberations for the rest of the century.

World War I set the stage for the dismantling of empires on both sides. For example, during the 1800s it had been said of England that the sun never set on the British Empire. But with the devastating casualties and material losses of World War I, British glory began to fade, a gradual process hastened by World War II only twenty years later. The Austro-Hungarian Empire suffered an even worse fate after World War I when, as a defeated power, it was carved up into several smaller nations that never regained the power and dominance of the empire they replaced. The Russian monarchy was severely weakened by the deprivations and horrendous casualties of the war. Russian revolutionaries supported by a desperate peasantry staged a massive revolt that deposed the czar and replaced the ancient monarchy. Unfortunately for the people of Russia, they had exchanged one form of oppression for another in the form of communism.

Finally, the Ottoman Empire, centered in modern-day Turkey, had at one time controlled North Africa, most of the Middle East, and southeastern Europe. By 1900, however, it was called the "sick man of Europe." World War I brought about its collapse when the Ottomans chose to fight on the side of Germany and

People celebrate Germany's surrender in November 1918, which ended the fighting during World War I.

Austria-Hungary in an attempt to regain lost territory. After the war the victorious Allies (Great Britain, France, Italy, and the United States, primarily) broke up the empire, creating many of the modern Arab nations. Further fragmented by nationalist movements, the region never regained a central power base.

But World War I brought positive changes for one country—the United States—which stepped into the international scene in a big way. In 1900 the United States was a minor player in world politics dominated by European powers such as England, France, and Germany. Early in the century, President Theodore Roosevelt prepared the nation for a bigger role in international politics when he urged a naval buildup, oversaw the creation of the Panama Canal, and received the Nobel Peace Prize for helping end a war between Japan and Russia. Officially neutral for most of World War I, the United States entered the conflict in April 1917 as a result of unrestricted German submarine warfare and contributed to the final defeat of Germany and its allies. While its European counterparts were exhausted by four years of fighting, the United States came out of the war relatively unscathed. Because no destruction had come to the United States, its economy and infrastructure remained fully functional and able to begin a postwar economic boom while Europe was left to rebuild shattered cities and economies.

One political legacy of World War I cast a large shadow over the remainder of the century. The victors of the war, including Great Britain, France, Italy, and the United States, dictated the terms of the formal peace treaty with the defeated Germany. Instead of creating a lasting peace, the Versailles Treaty imposed impossible requirements on Germany and its people, including enormous reparation payments and continued occupation of large amounts of its territory. Germany was incapable of making the payments, and its economy crumbled, prolonging the suffering of its people and causing long-term resentment of the Allies. German anger and bitterness proved to be fertile ground for the rise of Adolf Hitler, who promised to restore his country's pride and dignity during the 1930s. Fortunately, the treaty's grim legacy proved useful after World War II, when peace treaties allowed Germany and Japan to receive honorable terms and recover to become vibrant democracies.

The turbulent era between 1900 and 1920 marked a division between old world politics and new politics. A young nation called the United States came to dominate the world as older, more sophisticated nations faded from glory and power.

Sigmund Freud Publishes *The Interpretation of Dreams:* 1900

Freud Reveals the Unconscious Mind

by Robert B. Downs

Sigmund Freud revolutionized the study of the human mind. It was Freud who focused on the hidden, subconscious part of the mind, causing changes in psychiatry, education, therapy, and sociology. Along with Charles Darwin and Karl Marx, Freud influenced millions of twentieth-century people in Western society, for good or ill, according to critics or admirers.

The following selection, written by Robert B. Downs, a former president of the American Library Association and head of the University of Illinois Library, analyzes the one book Freud picked as his favorite work, *The Interpretation of Dreams*, published in 1900. Downs discusses Freud's basic ideas as presented in this early book and the resulting influence Freud's ideas had on the world.

F reud was one of the most prolific scientific writers of our time, and the variety of new concepts and psychological contributions which emanated from his pen cannot be found in any single book or paper. In his own eyes, probably the favorite was his earliest major work, *The Interpretation of Dreams*, issued in 1900, which contains nearly all of his fundamental observations and ideas. . . .

Freud and the Unconscious

Most critics would agree that Freud's claim to enduring fame rests on his discovery and exploration of the unconscious mind. Comparing the human mind to an iceberg, eight-ninths of which

Robert B. Downs, *Books That Changed the World*. New York: New American Library, 1956.

is submerged, he held that the mind is mainly hidden in the unconscious. Beneath the surface there are motives, feelings, and purposes which the individual conceals not only from others but even from himself. In Freudian psychology, the unconscious is supreme and conscious activity is reduced to a subordinate position. By coming to understand the profound and unknown depths of the unconscious, we learn the inner nature of man. Most of our thinking, declared Freud, is unconscious and only occasionally becomes conscious. The unconscious mind is the source of neuroses, because the individual tries to banish to that region his disagreeable memories and frustrated wishes, but only succeeds in storing them up for future trouble.

Freud classified mental activity in an individual as being carried on at three levels, which he named the Id, the Ego, and the Superego. Of first importance is the Id. "The domain of the Id," said Freud, "is the dark, inaccessible part of our personality; the little that we know of it we have learned through the study of dreams and of the formation of neurotic symptoms." The Id is the center of primitive instincts and impulses, reaching back to man's animal past, and is animal and sexual in nature. It is unconscious. The Id, continued Freud, "contains everything that is inherited, that is present at birth, that is fixed in the constitution." The Id is blind and ruthless, its sole purpose the gratification of desires and pleasures, without reckoning the consequences. In Thomas Mann's words, "It knows no values, no good or evil, no morality."

The new-born infant is the personification of the Id. Gradually, the Ego develops out of the Id as the child grows older. Instead of being guided entirely by the pleasure principle, the Ego is governed by the reality principle. The Ego is aware of the world around it, recognizing that the lawless tendencies of the Id must be curbed to prevent conflict with the rules of society. As Freud put it, the Ego is the mediator "between the reckless claims of the Id and the checks of the outer world." In effect, therefore, the Ego acts as censor of the Id's urges, adapting them to realistic situations, realizing that avoidance of punishment, or even self-preservation, may depend upon such repressions. Out of conflicts between the Ego and the Id, however, may develop neuroses seriously affecting the individual personality.

Finally, there is the third element in the mental process, the Superego, which may be broadly defined as conscience. The leading Freudian disciple in America, A.A. Brill, wrote:

> The Super-Ego is the highest mental evolution attainable by man, and consists of a precipitate of all prohibitions, all the rules of conduct which are impressed on the child by his parents and parental substitutes. The feeling of *conscience* depends altogether on the development of the Super-Ego.

Like the Id, the Superego is unconscious, and the two are in perpetual conflict, with the Ego acting as referee. Moral ideals and rules of behavior have the Superego as their home.

When the Id, Ego, and Superego are in reasonable harmony, the individual is well adjusted and happy. If the Ego permits the Id to break the rules, however, the Superego causes worry, feelings of guilt, and other manifestations of conscience.

Closely associated with the Id, is another concept originated by Freud: his theory of the *libido*. All the Id's impulses, he taught, are charged with a form of "psychic energy," termed *libido*, primarily sexual in character. The libido theory has been called "the essence of psychoanalytic doctrine." All man's cultural achievements, art, law, religion, etc., are regarded as developments of libido. While referred to as sexual energy, actually the word "sexual" is used in a very broad sense. In infants, it includes such activities as thumb-sucking, bottle-nursing, and excreting. In later years, the libido may be transferred to another person through marriage, take the form of sex perversion, or be expressed through artistic, literary, or musical creation—a process entitled "displacement." The sex instinct, in Freud's opinion, is the greatest source of creative work.

Under the influence of libido, Freud maintained, in perhaps the most controversial of all psychoanalytic theories, the child develops sexual feelings toward its parents. Beginning with its first sensual pleasures derived from feeding at the maternal breast, the infant forms a love attachment for its mother. As he matures, but at an early age, the male child develops strong sexual urges for the mother, while hating and fearing his father as a rival. The female child, on the other hand, may move away from the close relationship with her mother and fall in love with her father, with the mother becoming an object of dislike and rivalry. As applied to the male, this is called the Oedipus complex, named after the ancient Greek mythological figure, who killed his father and married his own mother. The Oedipus complex, Freud said, is a heritage from our primitive ancestors, who killed their fathers in jealous rages. As he reaches maturity, a normal person outgrows the Oedipus impulses. Weak individuals, on the other hand, may never succeed in breaking the parental attachment, and thus are led into a series of neuroses.

In fact, Freud declared, "The neuroses are without exception disturbances of the sexual function." Furthermore, neuroses cannot be blamed upon unsuccessful marriages or unfortunate adult love affairs, but all can be traced back to sex complexes of early childhood. Applying his theory to the field of anthropology, in his book *Totem and Taboo*, Freud concluded that nature and religious myths of primitive man are the product of father and mother complexes. Religion itself, he believed, is merely an expression of the father complex. After detailed analyses of hundreds of cases who came to him for treatment, Freud elevated sexual instinct and sexual desires to a pre-eminent role in the shaping of personality, as well as being the chief cause of neuroses. . . .

Because he is forced by society to suppress many of his urges, the individual unconsciously accumulates many "repressions," to use Freud's term. Normally, one's consciousness succeeds in preventing the "dark unconscious forces" that have been repressed from again emerging. Neurotic persons, though, may go through periods of deep emotional disturbances because of such censorship. It is the task of psychoanalytic therapy, said Freud, to "uncover repressions and replace them by acts of judgment which might result either in the acceptance or in the rejection of what had formerly been repudiated." Because of the painful nature of the repressed material, the patient usually tries to prevent the uncovering of his repressions. Freud termed these efforts "resistances," which it is the physician's object to overcome.

Therapy

The technique invented by Freud for dealing with repressions and resistances is the method now known as "free association"— stream-of-consciousness talk by a patient reclining on the psychoanalyst's couch, in a dimly lighted room. The patient is encouraged "to say whatever comes into his head, while ceasing to give any conscious direction to his thoughts." It was claimed by Freud that the method of free association is the only effective way of treating neurosis, and that it "achieved what was expected of it, namely the bringing into consciousness of the repressed material which was held back by resistances." As Brill described Freud's procedure with patients, "He persuaded them to give up all conscious reflection, abandon themselves to calm concentration, follow their spontaneous mental occurrences, and impart everything to him. In this way he finally obtained those *free associations* which lead to the origin of the symptoms." The forgotten material, dredged up by the subject out of his unconscious, after perhaps months of psychoanalytical treatment, usually represents something painful, disagreeable, frightening, or otherwise obnoxious out of his past, matters he dislikes to remember consciously.

Inevitably, in such a process, the rambling reminiscences produce a mass of diffuse, irrelevant, and apparently useless data. Everything, therefore, depends upon the ability of the physician to psychoanalyze his material, which, as various critics have pointed out, can be interpreted in an almost infinite number of ways. The intelligence and skill of the psychoanalyst, therefore, are of basic significance.

In the course of psychoanalytic treatment of patients, Freud discovered what he called "a factor of undreamt-of importance," an intense emotional relationship between the subject and the analyst. This is called "transference."

> The patient is not satisfied with regarding the analyst in the light of reality as a helper and adviser . . . on the contrary, the patient sees in his analyst the return—the reincarnation—of some important figure out of his childhood or past, and consequently transfers on to him feelings and reactions that undoubtedly applied to this model.

The transference "can vary between the extremes of a passionate, completely sensual love and the unbridled expression of an embittered defiance and hatred." In this situation, the analyst, "as a rule, is put in the place of one or other of the patient's parents, his father or his mother." The fact of transference, Freud regarded as "the best instrument of the analytic treatment," but "nevertheless its handling remains the most difficult as well as the most important part of the technique of analysis." The problem "is resolved," stated Freud, "by convincing the patient that he is re-experiencing emotional relations which had their origin in early childhood."

Another fruitful device for probing into inner conflicts and emotions developed by Freud was the analysis of dreams. Here again Freud was a pioneer. Before his time, dreams were regarded as without meaning or purpose. His *The Interpretation of*

Dreams was the first attempt at a serious scientific study of the phenomenon. Thirty-one years after publication of the book, Freud remarked that "It contains, even according to my present-day judgment, the most valuable of all the discoveries it has been my good fortune to make." According to Freud, "We are justified in asserting that a dream is the disguised fulfillment of a repressed wish." Each dream represents a drama in the inner world. "Dreams are invariably the product of a conflict," stated Freud, and "The dream is the guardian of sleep." Its function is to aid rather than disturb sleep, releasing tensions that come from unattainable wishes.

The dream world, in the Freudian view, is dominated by the unconscious, by the Id, and dreams are important to the psychoanalyst because they lead him into the patient's unconscious. In the unconscious are all the primitive wishes and emotional desires suppressed from conscious life by the Ego and Superego. The animal desires are always present under the surface, and force themselves forward in dreams. Even in sleep, however, the Ego and Superego stand on guard as censors. For that reason, the meanings of dreams are not always clear, they are expressed in symbols, and require expert interpretation. As symbols, they cannot be taken literally, except perhaps in the simple dreams of children. *The Interpretation of Dreams* offers numerous examples of dreams psychoanalyzed by Freud.

Likewise indicative of the workings of the unconscious are misspellings, slips of the tongue, and odd tricks of absent mindedness. "In the same way that psychoanalysis makes use of dream-interpretation," said Freud, "it also profits by the numerous little slips and mistakes which people make—symptomatic actions, as they are called." The subject was investigated by Freud in 1904 in his *The Psychopathology of Everyday Life.* In this work, he maintained that "these phenomena are not accidental . . . they have a meaning and can be interpreted, and one is justified in inferring from them the presence of restrained or repressed impulses and intentions." To forget a name may mean that one dislikes the person with that name. If a man misses his train because of confusion over schedules, it may indicate he did not desire to catch it. A husband who loses or forgets his house key may be unhappy at home and not desire to return. A study of such blunders can lead the psychoanalyst into the mazes of the unconscious mind.

The same release is obtained with jokes, which Freud termed "the best safety valve modern man has evolved," for through them we are temporarily freed of repressions that polite society otherwise requires us to keep hidden.

Perhaps because of premonitions, increasing disillusionment, or extreme pessimism, toward the end of his life, Freud became preoccupied with the "death instinct." Eventually, he came to regard this conception as almost on a par in importance with the sexual instinct. Freud held that there is a death instinct driving all living matter to return to the inorganic state from which it came. According to this view, man is constantly torn between the urge to life, that is the sexual instinct, and a counter force, the urge to annihilation, or the death instinct. In the end, of course, the death instinct wins out. The instinct is responsible for war, and for such examples of sadism as prejudice against races and classes, the vicarious enjoyment of criminal trials, bullfighting, and lynching.

The foregoing, in brief, are the principal facets of Freudian theory. Present-day psychiatrists are split into two or more opposing camps, pro and anti Freud. Even his disciples have modified their full acceptance of the theories over the past fifty years. One of the early followers, Alfred Adler, seceded from the Freudian camp because he believed that Freud had overemphasized the sexual instincts. As an alternative doctrine, Adler taught that every man's desire to prove his superiority is the mainspring in human behavior. He developed the idea of an "inferiority complex" which impels the individual to strive for recognition in some activity. Another famous secessionist was Karl Jung, of Zurich, who also tried to minimize the role of sex. Jung divided mankind into two psychological types: extroverts and introverts, though he recognized that every individual is a mixture of the two. Unlike Freud, Jung emphasized hereditary factors in the development of personality. In general, Freud's critics part company with him on such issues as his insistence on the prime significance of childhood neuroses, his conviction that men are controlled by primeval, rigid instincts, and on his elevating the libido or sexual energy to a central place in the formation of personality. Some disagree with Freud also in his belief that free association is an infallible technique for exploring the unconscious, pointing out most particularly the difficulties in interpreting data produced by that method.

Freud's Significance

Nevertheless, as one psychiatrist observed:

> The changes and developments of sixty years have in no way diminished Freud's stature or influence. He opened up the realm of the unconscious. He showed how it helps to make us what we are and how to reach it. Many of his ideas and concepts have had to be modified by his successors in the light of further experience. You might say that they have been writing a New Testament for psychiatry. But Sigmund Freud wrote the Old Testament. His work will remain basic.

Much of our modern attitude toward insanity we owe to Freud. There is an increasing tendency to suggest that "Neurotics and psychotics are just like ourselves, only more so." Alexander Reid Martin stressed that "Whether acknowledged or not, all psychiatric and psychotherapeutic hospitals today utilize elements and fundamentals of Freudian psychology. What formerly was regarded as an unknown world, forbidding, grotesque, purposeless and meaningless, through Freud became enlightened and charged with meaning, attracting the interest and recognition not only of medicine, but of all the social sciences."

The impact of Freudian thought on literature and art has been equally noticeable. In fiction, poetry, drama, and other literary forms, Freudian motifs have flourished in recent years. Bernard De Voto has expressed the opinion that "no other scientist has ever had so strong and so widespread an influence on literature." The effect on painting, sculpture, and the world of art in general has been no less profound.

To sum up the manifold contribution of Freud's genius is difficult because of the breadth of his interests and the controversial nature of his findings. One attempt was made by an English writer, Robert Hamilton, whose conclusion was this:

> Freud put psychology on the map. He was a great pioneer and much of his success was due to his originality and literary style. In spite of its nihilistic character, there has never been a system more interesting and original, nor, outside pure literature, a more attractive style. He made the world think psychologically—an essential need for our time; and he forced men to ask themselves questions vital to human welfare. Out of the thesis of the sterile academic psychology of the nineteenth century he brought the antithesis of psycho-analysis with its dark negations.

A noted American psychiatrist, Frederic Wertham, stated the case from another point of view:

> One should make clear that, aside from the host of new clinical facts about patients that he observed, Freud brought about three fundamental changes in the approach to the study of personality and mental pathology. The first was to speak of psychological processes at all, and to think of them with the logic of natural science. This became possible only when Freud introduced the realistic concept of the unconscious and practical methods for its investigation. The second was his introduction of a new dimension into psychopathology: childhood. Before Freud, psychiatry was practiced as if every patient was Adam—who never was a child. The third was his inauguration of the genetic understanding of the sexual instinct. His real discovery here was not so much that children have a sex life, but that the sexual instinct has a childhood.

A similar judgment was expressed by A.G. Tansley, in an obituary prepared for the Royal Society of London:

> The revolutionary nature of Freud's conclusions becomes intelligible when we remember that he was investigating an entirely unexplored field, a region of the human mind into which no one had penetrated before, and whose overt manifestations had been regarded as inexplicable or as degenerative aberrations, or had been ignored because they lay under the strongest human taboos. The very existence of this field was unrecognized. Freud was forced to assume the reality of an unconscious region of the mind, and then to attempt to explore it, by the apparent discontinuities in the chains of conscious mental events.

Finally, Winfred Overholser suggests that "There is every reason to think that one hundred years hence Freud will be classed with Copernicus and Newton as one of the men who opened up new vistas of thought. Certain it is that in our time no man has cast so much light upon the workings of the mind of man as Freud."

The last months of Freud's long lifetime were spent in exile. Following the Nazi occupation of Austria, he was forced to leave Vienna in 1938. England granted him asylum, but cancer of the mouth caused his death in September 1939, a little more than a year later.

Marconi Sends the First Wireless Signal Across the Atlantic: December 12, 1901

Marconi Overturns Scientific Skepticism

by Degna Marconi

Degna Marconi, the oldest child of Guglielmo Marconi, wrote the definitive personal biography of the famous inventor and businessman. In the following selection she tells of his success at becoming the first person to bridge the Atlantic by wireless. Up until this time, communication across the oceans was accomplished by cable, an expensive and limited method that involved huge ships and extended periods of time.

In 1896, Marconi had left Italy for England because it was a hub of trade and industry. There he created the world's first wireless system of telegraphy. He soon became a celebrity and set up a company to make use of the invention. He went on to demonstrate the value of wireless to protect lives at sea by means of ship-to-shore communication. The British Admiralty was impressed enough to ask Marconi to fit three Royal Navy ships with wireless for its first use during naval maneuvers. While visiting the United States, he established his company's American subsidiary, which eventually became the Radio Corporation of America (RCA). It was at this time, in 1901, that Marconi took on a scientific and economic gamble by trying to bridge the Atlantic by wireless.

In this selection Marconi's daughter, Degna, describes the attempt. Marconi decided to use a site at Signal Hill, located in St. John's, Newfoundland, Canada. His other site, which would send

Degna Marconi, *My Father, Marconi*. New York: McGraw-Hill, 1962.

the message, was set up at Poldhu in Cornwall, England. Marconi sailed to Newfoundland in November 1901 with two assistants and his equipment. Against the advice of scientists and inventors who believed radio waves would not be able to travel over the earth's curved surface, Marconi prepared for the difficult test. His daughter describes the tension as the test proceeded and the joy at the results.

s they sailed into St. John's, the three scientific voyagers at the rail had been struck by the tower to John Cabot which stands high above the harbor.

Preparations

"After taking a look at various sites which might prove suitable, I considered that the best one was to be found on Signal Hill, a lofty eminence overlooking the port and forming the natural bulwark which protects it from the fury of the Atlantic gales. On top of the hill there is a small plateau of some two acres in area which I thought very suitable for the manipulation of either the balloons or the kites. On the crag of this plateau rose the new Cabot Memorial Tower which was designed as a signal station, and close to it there was an old military barracks which was then used as a hospital."

Beside this two-story stone building is a walled courtyard nakedly exposed to the weather, where the *Herald* man found them. As a result of his visit he sent a story his paper published the next day, Tuesday, December 10. Marconi and his assistants, he said matter-of-factly, were busy unpacking instruments and removing the balloons and several cylinders of hydrogen gas to one of the old buildings near the tower. A local firm was about to prepare the ground by covering it with zinc.

When Marconi picked up the story, the tone was very different. "It was in a room in this building that I set up my apparatus and made preparations for the great experiment." Two hundred and twenty-five miles had been bridged by wireless between Poldhu and Crookhaven. Now it was 2,170 that he proposed to put to the test.

"On Monday, December nine, barely three days after my arrival, I began work on Signal Hill, together with my assistants." He had not lost the old habit of sharing credit, working as lead man of a team. "I had decided to try one of the balloons first as a means of elevating the aerial and by Wednesday we had inflated it and it made its first ascent in the morning. Its diameter was about fourteen feet and it contained 1,000 cubic feet of hydrogen gas, quite sufficient to hold up the aerial which consisted of a wire weighing about ten pounds."

As the *Herald* described it: "Mr. Marconi was at Signal Hill all day testing the balloons. . . . He hopes to have everything completed by Thursday or Friday, when he will try and communicate with the Cunard steamer *Lucania*, which left Liverpool on Saturday." The disguise was working perfectly.

"The experiments are exciting keen interest here," he went on. "St. John's merchants are considering the advisability of having the system installed on the sealing steamers.

"It is reported that the Canadian Government is awaiting results of Mr. Marconi's experiments here preparatory to having the system installed along the entrance to the Gulf of St. Lawrence."

Tuesday was difficult. The captive balloon was launched but escaped. Wednesday's account in the *Herald* described what happened: "Mr. Marconi lost a balloon today while experimenting for the proposed wireless signals here. 'Although foggy, the weather did not look unfavorable for our work,' Mr. Marconi said, 'and we continued experiments. One of the balloons measuring fourteen feet in diameter was sent up. The wind freshened quickly increasing to a gale, and when the balloon had gone up about one hundred feet we decided to take it down. Unfortunately the rope broke and it disappeared out at sea.'"

"'Today's accident will delay us for a few days and it will not be possible to communicate with a Cunarder this week. I hope, however, to do so next week, possibly with the steamer leaving New York on Saturday,'" the *Herald* quoted him as saying.

Father's and Paget's [Marconi's assistant] account, given later over BBC, makes it clear that this was not the whole story: ". . . the weather," Paget recalled, "was terrible and for a couple of days we battled with the elements, one of the balloons having been carried away by the gale, which snapped the heavy mooring rope like a piece of cotton. So Mr. Marconi suggested that for his crucial test on the third day we should use kites, and on that morning we managed to fly a kite up to four hundred feet.

"It flew over the stormy Atlantic, surged up and down in the gale tugging at its six hundred foot aerial wire. The icy rain lashed my face as I watched it anxiously. The wind howled around the building where in a small dark room furnished with a table, one chair and some packing cases, Mr. Kemp sat at the receiving set while Mr. Marconi drank a cup of cocoa before taking his turn at listening for the signals which were being transmitted from Poldhu, at least we hoped so."

Success

Father takes up the story: "It was shortly after midday on December 12, 1901, that I placed a single earphone to my ear and started listening. The receiver on the table before me was very crude—a few coils and condensers and a coherer, no valves, no amplifier, not even a crystal.

"I was at last on the point of putting the correctness of all my beliefs to the test. The experiment had involved risking at least 50,000 pounds to achieve a result which had been declared impossible by some of the principal mathematicians of the time. The chief question was whether wireless waves could be stopped by the curvature of the earth. All along I had been convinced that this was not so, but some eminent men held that the roundness of the earth would prevent communication over such a great distance as across the Atlantic. The first and final answer to that question came at 12:30."

He set down exactly what happened then.

"Suddenly, about half past twelve there sounded the sharp click of the 'tapper' as it struck the coherer, showing me that something was coming and I listened intently.

"Unmistakably, the three sharp clicks corresponding to three dots sounded in my ear; but I would not be satisfied without corroboration.

"'Can you hear anything, Mr. Kemp?' I said, handing the telephone to my assistant. Kemp heard the same thing as I.P.W. Paget, a little deaf, was unable to hear it, and I knew then that I had been absolutely right in my calculations. The electric waves which were being sent out from Poldhu had traveled the Atlantic, serenely ignoring the curvature of the earth which so many doubters considered would be a fatal obstacle, and they were now affecting my receiver in Newfoundland. I knew that the day on which I should be able to send full messages without wires or cables across the Atlantic was not far-distant."

In this triumphant hour, his vision of the future did not include the frantic battles that would ensue with the cable company.

"The distance had been overcome and further development of the sending and receiving apparatus was all that was required.

"After a short while the signals stopped, evidently owing to changes in the capacity of the aerial which in turn were due to the varying height of the kite. But again at 1:10 and 1:20 the three sharp little clicks were distinctly and unmistakably heard, about twenty-five times altogether.

"On Saturday a further attempt was made to obtain a repetition of the signals but owing to difficulties with the kite we had to give up the attempt. However, there was no further doubt possible that the experiment had succeeded and that afternoon, December 14, I sent a cablegram to Major Flood Page, managing director of the Marconi Company, informing him that the signals had been received but that the weather made continuous tests extremely difficult. The same night I also gave the news to the press at St. John's whence it was telegraphed to all parts of the world." That very day he also cabled the news to Pontecchio.

The New York Times began its December 15 story on this extraordinary piece of news: "St. John's, N.F. Dec. 14.—Guglielmo Marconi announced tonight the most wonderful scientific development of modern times."

And what of the *Herald?* Its reporter's interest seems to have flagged on the crucial Thursday and Friday, for his Saturday story opened: "The weather on Signal Hill was extremely cold and unfavorable for wireless telegraphy experiments. The kite used yesterday fell into the water near the cliff, but was afterward rescued by a passing tug-boat and returned."

Results

He had missed the scoop.

Now the world knew and congratulations poured in. Small girls, in chilly little clumps, climbed Signal Hill with bouquets of flowers for Father. The Governor gave a lunch with long speeches on the historic role of Newfoundland as the link between Europe and America. Everyone was interviewed. Professor Michael Pupin, American scientist and inventor, acknowledged handsomely that "Marconi has proved conclusively that the curvature of the earth is no obstacle to the system of wireless telegraphy." In New York, Mr. Cuthbert Hall of the Marconi Company received reporters and prophesied that there was no foreseeable limit to the number of messages that could be exchanged by wireless and tactlessly compared the costs of wireless installations to the costs of laying cable (there were by now fourteen on the Atlantic bed, enough to girdle the earth seven times).

This brought an immediate dissent from the president of the Commercial Cable Company. "Signor Marconi," he said, "had mistaken the action of the ground current or lightning for signals."

But the lay public was delighted. They still saw Marconi as a boy and even more delightful, as a boy with a kite. Ray Stannard Baker, writing for *McClure's*, caught this reaction: "A cable, marvelous as it is, maintains a tangible and material connection between speaker and hearer: one can grasp its meaning. But here is nothing but space, a pole with a pendant wire on one side of a broad and curving ocean, an uncertain kite struggling in the air on the other—and thought passing between. And the apparatus for sending and receiving these transoceanic messages costs not a thousandth part of the expense of a cable. . . .

"The portrait published with this article, taken at St. John's a few days after the experiments, gives a very good idea of the inventor's face, though it cannot convey the peculiar lustre of his eyes when he is interested or excited—and perhaps it makes him look older than he really is. One of the first and strongest impressions that the man conveys is that of intense activity and mental absorption. He talks little, is straightforward and unassuming, submitting good-naturedly—although with evident unwillingness—to be lionized."

In the eyes of the world what Marconi had done with two balloons and six kites was magic, an occult modern mystery. The Field achievement was by comparison pedestrian and cumbersome. He himself had written when he was taken aboard the *Great Eastern* to see the ship's crew through their heavy labors, toward the end of the cable-laying voyage, that there had been on board "ten bullocks, one milk cow, 114 sheep, 20 pigs, 29 geese, 14 turkeys, 500 fowls as live stock and dead stock in larger numbers, including 28 bullocks and eighteen thousand eggs." Nor was this all. When they dragged the ocean floor to bring up the "slimy monster," they had to use as grapnel twenty miles of rope twisted with wires of steel in order to bear the strain imposed by thirty tons of cable. It took two hours even to lower it to the bottom. As against this, Marconi had instantaneously caught his intangible train of waves with a kite that could be packed in a wicker hamper and weighed a few ounces.

Long, long afterward, the Italian government asked my father to record, in his own voice, the thing he accomplished in Newfoundland. I listened to the record in the Library of Congress in Washington, D.C. It had been years since he had heard the three dots come over the stormy sea from Poldhu but the excitement is there, fresh and real, beneath the controlled, musical voice.

Marconi's Legacy Impacted the Way the World Sent Messages

by the Marconi Corporation

Marconi, the communications company founded by the inventor himself, has a website that explains much of Guglielmo Marconi's work. In the following piece taken from the company's description of their founder, Marconi's breakthroughs are discussed. It starts with the reaction of his famous experiment in 1901 when he sent and received a wireless signal that traveled across the entire Atlantic Ocean, thus proving that radio waves were not stopped by the curvature of the earth as some had predicted. After his transatlantic success, he set up a number of stations to communicate with ships at sea and eventually was credited with saving many lives threatened by disasters at sea. In addition, his device was used by police to catch a dangerous criminal. In World War I his company supported the Allied cause in many ways. Wireless, in the form of radio, became a popular source of entertainment. It was Marconi and others who formed the British Broadcasting Corporation (BBC) in the late 1920s. He was also involved in the development of radar and television.

With total justification Guglielmo Marconi is called the pioneer of wireless, freeing communications from the constraints imposed by fixed cable and visible distance. Conquering distance, he facilitated commercial and mass communication, bringing all parts of the world closer together. In an era when all intercontinental transport was entirely marine, Marconi's achievements in wireless meant that ships at sea were no longer isolated and beyond reach of communication once they left sight of land. Marconi personally was regarded as a great benefactor and was accorded recognition and decorations wherever he went. . . .

The British press was sceptical [of his 1901 experiment] as were many scientists. But in North America the Canadian government hailed Marconi as a benefactor and offered him land plus £16,000 towards building a wireless station there. In New York he was honoured by the American Institute of Electrical Engineers, and by Alexander Graham Bell and Thomas Edison personally. Shares in cable companies dipped sharply; but Marconi returned to England with his case unproven.

In February 1902, however, Marconi sailed once more for the USA on board the SS *Philadelphia*, which had been fitted with aerials attached to the ship's masts. As the ship steamed westwards signals were sent from Poldhu and came through clearly on the Morse tape inker. The captain attested that readable messages were received up to 1,551 miles at sea. Reception of the Morse code for the letter 'S' was maintained on the filings coherer up to 2,099 miles. All this was achieved using aerial masts of 150 feet, as against the kite-supported aerial at St John's of 500 feet.

Marconi Sets Up Stations

At last sceptics were silenced. By the end of 1902 Marconi had established a permanent station at Glace Bay in Nova Scotia, Canada, as well as at Cape Cod in the USA. Messages were sent in December from the Governor General of Canada and Marconi to King Edward VII, also from Marconi to the King of Italy. In January 1903, the first wireless message to be transmitted directly from the USA to England was sent from the President to King Edward VII.

By 1903, the Company had built a number of stations on shore and many merchant ships had been fitted with its wireless sets, which had to be rented from the company and were operated by

Marconi personnel, who were allowed to communicate with operators using apparatus from rival companies during emergencies only. As a result of the growing maritime business the Company began to make a profit. . . .

Successes at Sea

In 1909, Marconi shared the credit when 1,700 lives were saved through wireless distress calls when two liners collided and one of them sank off the coast of the USA. He then shared the Nobel Prize for Physics with one of the founders of his company's rival, the Telefunken company of Germany.

In July 1910, Marconi enjoyed success again when the wireless was sensationally applied for the first time to apprehend a dangerous criminal. On the westward bound SS *Montrose*, the captain asked his Marconi operator to send a brief message to England: "Have strong suspicions that Crippen London cellar murderer and accomplice are among saloon passengers. Accomplice dressed as boy. Voice manner and build undoubtedly a girl." A detective from Scotland Yard boarded a faster ship and arrested him before the SS *Montrose* docked in Montreal.

Soon it was mandatory for every large ship to be equipped with wireless and have at least one operator, but even this could not prevent accidents happening. On the night of 14 April 1912, on her maiden voyage to New York, the liner, SS *Titanic*, deemed unsinkable, struck an iceberg and sank, with the loss of some 1,500 lives. Among them was one of the two Marconi wireless operators, whose distress signals nevertheless brought rescue to over 700 survivors. "Those who have been saved," said the British Postmaster-General, "have been saved through one man, Mr Marconi . . . and his wonderful invention.". . .

Marconi During World War I

Marconi was in England at the outbreak of the First World War in August 1914. When Italy chose neutrality he was classified in Britain as an alien but the government permitted him to leave after first requisitioning his company's sites.

Company personnel played a significant part in every aspect and theatre of conflict from training army signallers to developing air-to-ground and air-to-air telegraphy and equipping 600 planes of the Royal Flying Corps; from building shore stations for the Royal Navy to setting up a direction-finding (DF) chain for locating enemy Zeppelins and submarines; from providing a lifeline for merchant ships to tracking the German fleet before the Battle of Jutland. . . .

Further Results

Meanwhile, wireless rapidly became a popular new source of home entertainment. Dame Nellie Melba sang during Britain's first advertised public broadcast programme from Chelmsford in June 1920. In 1922, programmes, from a temporary studio near Chelmsford with the call sign 2MT and from 2LO at Marconi House in London, attracted so many listeners that a new subsidiary, Marconiphone, was set up to manufacture and sell broadcast receivers. Government intervention led Marconi and his largest competitors to join forces and establish the British Broadcasting Company (BBC), which, in 1927, became the British Broadcasting Corporation. . . .

Between 1931 and 1935, returning to his earliest research at Villa Griffone, Marconi experimented with microwaves. At sea, aboard the *Elettra* in 1934, he used this technique for blind navigation by radio beacon. This was a precursor of radar, developed, thanks to him and others, for Britain's defence in the Second World War.

In 1936, C.S. Franklin, an engineer employed by Marconi since 1899, designed the massive aerial tower at Alexandra Palace in north London, for the BBC's first high-definition television transmitter, an invention foreseen many years before by Campbell-Swinton, who had introduced Marconi to William Preece, the most influential of his supporters. Prophetic words, spoken by Preece 40 years earlier, had come true: "Marconi has produced a new system . . . that will reach places hitherto inaccessible."

Guglielmo Marconi died in Rome on 20 July 1937. In a gesture that was unique among all the tributes that followed, wireless stations closed down and transmitters all over the world fell silent. The ether was as quiet as it had been before Marconi was born.

William McKinley's Assassination Leads to Roosevelt's Presidency

by Nathan Miller

Nathan Miller is a four-time nominee for the Pulitzer Prize. He is the author of *FDR: An Intimate History*, *The Roosevelt Chronicles*, and *The U.S. Navy*. In the following selection, Miller describes the assassination of William McKinley. This was an especially ironic turn of events for a couple of reasons. Roosevelt had been selected as vice president on the 1900 Republican ticket partially by some who did not like his independence and civic reforms. They thought that they would be ridding themselves of a headache by kicking him upstairs to vice president, a job where he could do no harm. Roosevelt himself thought that becoming vice president would take him out of active politics since the job had traditionally been low-key. However, as Miller points out, a young man shot McKinley in the summer of 1901 and catapulted Roosevelt to the presidency at the youthful age of forty-two.

Nathan Miller, *Theodore Roosevelt: A Life*. New York: William Morrow and Company, 1992. Copyright © 1992 by Nathan Miller. Reproduced by permission.

At the end of the summer [1901], both the president and the vice president embarked on tours of the country, letting themselves be seen by the American people. Roosevelt began a series of speaking engagements that took him, on September 6, to a meeting of the Vermont Fish and Game League on Isle La Motte in Lake Champlain. That same day, McKinley was winding up a two-day visit to the Pan American Exposition at Buffalo, a lavish international festival designed to dramatize progress in the Western Hemisphere. The vice president had already toured the exhibition, but the president had postponed his appearance because of his wife's poor health. Following a summer in Canton, the first lady now felt better, and he had happily brought her with him.

The Shooting of McKinley

While Mrs. McKinley was resting at the home of John G. Milburn, the exposition's president, McKinley attended a public reception at the ornate Temple of Music. Anyone who wished could shake the hand of the president as he stood in a bower of palm trees, and hundreds of people were waiting in line for the doors to open. Worried about the lack of security, George B. Cortelyou, the crisply efficient presidential secretary, tried to persuade McKinley to call off the reception, but the president refused. "Why should I?" he asked. "No one would want to hurt me."

The day was warm and as the line flowed along to the strains of an organ playing a Bach cantata, some people wiped their brows with handkerchiefs. With only minutes to go before the doors were shut, a young Polish-American named Leon Czolgosz approached the president. His right hand was wrapped in a handkerchief as though it were injured, and his left hand was extended instead. McKinley reached for it, but they never clasped hands. Czolgosz brought up his "bandaged" right hand, pressed it almost against the president's vest, and fired two shots from a concealed revolver.

Smoke curled from the "bandage," and the president sagged into the arms of shocked officials. Shouts and screams blended into a rapid blur of violence. The assassin was wrestled to the ground and pummeled by a falling avalanche of spectators and guards. "Go easy on him, boys," pleaded the president before lapsing into unconsciousness.

Vice President Roosevelt was preparing to attend a reception on Isle La Motte when the telephone rang. He was told the president had been shot by a man identified as an anarchist, and exploratory surgery was under way. No one yet knew the severity of McKinley's wounds, but the vice president was requested to come to Buffalo immediately. Roosevelt hurried to Burlington, where a special train was waiting. On the trip across the lake, someone remarked that he might at any moment become president of the United States. Roosevelt quickly rebuked the man by saying all thoughts ought to be of the stricken chief executive.

In Buffalo, Roosevelt learned that one of Czolgosz's bullets had ripped through the president's stomach, damaging the liver and pancreas before lodging in his back. The doctors were worried about gangrene, but there was no sign of infection. McKinley, who had been taken to the Milburn home, rallied following surgery and optimistic bulletins were issued about his condition. "The President is coming along splendidly," Roosevelt reported to his sister Bamie. "Awful though this crime was against the President it was a thousand-fold worse crime against this Republic and against free government all over the world."

On September 10, four days after the shooting, McKinley seemed to be out of danger, and Roosevelt was told he need not remain by the presidential bedside. In fact, aides believed the vice president's departure would help assure the nation that the crisis was over. Mark Hanna called McKinley's condition "just glorious" and went home to Cleveland. Roosevelt joined Edith and the children at a camp in the Adirondacks, near Mount Tahawus, where she had taken them in hopes that the cooler air would speed their recovery from various illnesses.

Three days later, the president unexpectedly took a turn for the worse and began drifting in and out of consciousness. "Is Mark there?" he asked several times, but Hanna had not yet returned to Buffalo. George Cortelyou dispatched a telegram to the vice president informing him of the alarming change in McKinley's condition. This was followed by messages urging him to come to Buffalo immediately. Occasionally, the stricken man regained consciousness long enough to murmur a few disconnected lines of his favorite hymn, "Nearer My God to Thee," and snatches of prayer. Hanna arrived at last and rushed to the side of his dying friend. "Mr. President, Mr. President," he called out to the pale figure. There was no sign of recognition in the glazed eyes. In his anguish, Hanna dropped all formality. "William! William!"

he cried out. "Don't you know me?"

The president's breathing grew labored and finally at 2:45 in the morning of September 14, it ceased entirely. One of the attending physicians, who had been listening to McKinley's heart, straightened up and quietly announced, "The President is dead."

Roosevelt Learns of McKinley's Death

For twelve suspenseful hours, the nation had no president. Unaware of the crisis, Roosevelt had spent September 13 with friends climbing Mount Marcy, the highest peak in the Adirondacks. The climb was exhausting, the clouds and rain so thick the climbers could not see ten feet ahead of them, and the rocks were slippery. When they reached the summit, the mist suddenly cleared, bathing them in sunshine. "Beautiful country!" Roosevelt declared as he gazed across the expanse of trees, lakes, and mountains that stretched to the horizon. "Beautiful country!" Just as quickly as it had cleared, however, the sky darkened and heavy clouds covered the vista like the sea.

On the way down, the party stopped to eat at a shelf of land where there was a little lake named Tear-of-the-Clouds. Roosevelt was just about to bite into a sandwich when he looked up and saw a guide on the trail leading up from below. "I had had a bully tramp and was looking forward to dinner with the interest only an appetite worked up in the woods gives you," he recalled. "When I saw the runner I instinctively knew he had bad news— the worst news in the world."

Upon reading Cortelyou's telegram, Roosevelt scrambled down the slope and hiked as fast as he could to the nearest telephone, located at the Tahawus Club, about a dozen miles away. Further reports confirmed the president's deteriorating condition, but curiously he did not leave for Buffalo for another four and a half hours. Why the delay? Edith supplied an answer several years later. "When the party came down from Mount Marcy, my husband came to me and he said, 'I'm not going unless I am really needed,'" she explained. "'I have been there once and that shows how I feel. But I will not go to stand beside those people who are suffering and anxious. I am going to wait here.'"

Word was received about ten o'clock that night that McKinley was dying. One of the children, who knew the president had been shot, began to cry because he was afraid his father would be shot, too, if he became president. A buckboard was hitched up, and Roosevelt and the driver set off on a wild ride to North Creek, forty miles away, where William Loeb, his secretary, was standing by with a special train. Bouncing against rocks, and sliding in the mud, they raced down a twisting wilderness trail where a wrong turn meant a plunge over a precipice.

"Faster!" Roosevelt cried to the driver. "Faster!" The buckboard was reined in only long enough to change horses and drivers, and then they were off again. Dawn was breaking as Roosevelt clattered up to the North Creek station. He jumped down from the mud-splattered vehicle to learn that McKinley had died during the night. By the flickering light of a kerosene lamp, he read the telegram informing him he was now president of the United States.

Throughout the trip across the breadth of New York State, the normally exuberant Roosevelt kept his own counsel. Perhaps he was thinking how many major crises of his life—the death of his father, the passing of Alice Lee—had found him in similar circumstances. Newsmen mobbed the train at Albany, Utica, Rome, and Syracuse, but he remained in seclusion. Earlier, he had sent a brief telegram to Edith whose formality spoke volumes:

> PRESIDENT MCKINLEY DIED AT 2:15 THIS MORNING.
> THEODORE ROOSEVELT

The special train reached Buffalo at 1:34 P.M. Wearing a top hat that Loeb had found somewhere, Roosevelt went to the Milburn house to pay his respects to the dead president and his family. Then he was driven to the home of Ansley Wilcox to await the swearing-in. A Buffalo policeman, Anthony J. Gavin, thrust his head into the carriage window. "Mr. Roosevelt," he asked, "will you shake hands with me?" Lost in thought, Roosevelt glanced up and then brightened. "Why, hello, Tony," he replied, "I'm glad to see you." There is no record indicating where they met, but the incident was a forecast of the astonishing range of presidential acquaintances that were soon to fascinate the nation.

As the senior member of the Cabinet present, Secretary of War Elihu Root was in charge of swearing in the new president. No one was certain of the proper procedure, so an aide was sent to the city library to consult newspaper accounts of the induction of Chester Arthur following the death of President Garfield. Shortly after three o'clock, Cabinet members, a few guests, and a handful of reporters gathered in the somber shadows of the

Wilcox library, amid the ghostly shapes of furniture still draped with summer dustcloths.

Roosevelt's eye was caught by a small bird perched on the windowsill, chirping and fluttering its wings, before turning his attention to Root. Voice choked with emotion, the war secretary suggested that he take the oath of office without delay. Roosevelt, his face stern and stiff, signaled his acquiescence with a slight bow and responded with words that were designed to allay national uncertainty and tensions: "The administration of the government will not falter in spite of the terrible blow. . . . It shall be my aim to continue, absolutely, unbroken, the policy of President McKinley for the peace, the prosperity, and the honor of our beloved country."

With his right arm held up in the air like a schoolboy who wished to be recognized, Roosevelt took the oath of office as twenty-sixth president of the United States. In repeating the words after Judge John R. Hazel, his high-pitched voice showed signs of nervousness at first, but by the time he reached a final "And so I swear"—a touch he added himself—the words rang out loud and clear.

Later he and Root went for a short walk. Just as they returned, a carriage rolled up to the Wilcox house. From it emerged Mark Hanna, bent with rheumatism and with his spirit crushed. William McKinley had been more than a friend and political ally, he had been his life. Long before Hanna reached the door, Roosevelt bounded down the steps, hand outstretched to greet him. For a moment, Hanna lost his composure and then, pulling himself together, said: "Mr. President, I wish you success and a prosperous administration. I trust you will command me if I can be of any service."

At forty-two, Theodore Roosevelt was now the youngest president in American history.

Theodore Roosevelt: First Modern President

by *Time*

Time magazine put out several special report issues during America's bicentennial celebration in 1976. In this issue, devoted to presidents of the United States, the writers discuss Roosevelt as the first modern president, thanks to his vitality, optimism, attack on greedy corporations, and interest in world peace. Most of all, he set the standard for future presidents by using the office as his "bully pulpit" to urge Americans to follow his ideas.

Theodore Roosevelt roared into the White House with the exploding vitality, the volcanic optimism, the flaming soul of the new century. He was the man who gave substance to the spirit of America that had been gathering from Concord Bridge to the Oregon Trail, from Gettysburg to "Remember the Maine!" He was the man who was to change the nation, change the world, and not just for the new century. "The world has set its face hopefully toward our democracy," said T.R. Nobody called him Teddy to his face. His eyes would ignite behind the steel-rimmed spectacles, his fists clench, his mustache bristle. His high voice propelled ballistically: "And, oh, my fellow citizens, *each—one— of—you*—carries on your shoulders the burden of doing well for the sake of your own country—and of seeing that this nation does well for the sake of mankind."

Specifically, Theodore Roosevelt, as President, went to work defining what kind of nation America ought to be: Jeffersonian for "genuine faith in democracy and popular government," and Hamiltonian for "the need of the exercise of broad powers by the national Government." He mobilized the American people to help put down robber industrialists and radical labor leaders precisely so he could protect—and project—both U.S. business and U.S. labor as U.S. institutions. "There had been a riot of individualistic materialism," and "malefactors of great wealth," but for doubt there would be faith, for "don't care" there would be dedication, and America for all time would be the land of opportunity to which the golden gates would never snap shut. America would become a new kind

Theodore Roosevelt

of country in which Americans would align "never between section and section, never between creed and creed, and never, thrice never, between class and class, *but—that—the—line—be—drawn*—on the line of conduct."

He was also the first U.S. President to mobilize the American people to work for the U.S. interest in world peace and order. "Speak softly and carry a big stick, you will go far," he counseled, and the new concept for the new century was deterrence. U.S. armed forces would be deployed with visible strength and efficiency for the first time, not just to win wars, but to discourage other nations from starting wars.

Finally, Theodore Roosevelt was the first U.S. President not only to envision but to enact measures for the conservation of national resources: "I do not recognize the right . . . to rob, by wasteful use, the generations that come after us." He appealed to the conscience of the nation as he set aside an incredible—at the time—150,000,000 acres of timberland for national use.

It was on October 27, 1858, that this President was born, son of a wealthy merchant-banker, at 28 East 20th Street in New York City. A frail, asthmatic youngster, he exercised so devotedly he was able to box at Harvard, where he graduated Phi Beta Kappa. Always oriented toward public service, he joined Manhattan's

21st District Republican Club and was elected and reelected as a reform member of the lower house of the New York State legislature. After the death of his first wife, Alice Lee, he headed west to work on the Maltese Cross and Elkhorn cattle ranches in the Badlands beneath the thunderclouds of the Dakota Territory. "Black care rarely sits behind a rider whose pace is fast enough," he explained.

Revitalized, T.R. wed a childhood playmate, Edith Kermit Carow, and they settled into Sagamore Hill, at Oyster Bay, Long Island, which was to be his beloved, trophy-cluttered, lifelong home. He served six years as a reform Civil Service Commissioner under Presidents Harrison and Cleveland. That was followed by two years as police commissioner of New York City, where he was deeply moved by his constant prowling on the beats through the slums. "I am dealing with the most important and yet most elementary problems of our municipal life," he wrote. "There is nothing of the purple in it. It is grimy."

Appointed by President McKinley in 1897 to serve as Assistant Secretary of the Navy, T.R. argued for war with Spain, not just to liberate Cuba, but to rally the U.S. into the kind of energetic world involvement advocated by Admiral Alfred Thayer Mahan, author of *The Influence of Sea Power Upon History*. As colonel of the 1st U.S. Volunteer Cavalry—the "Rough Riders"—he led the famous charge against the Spanish defenses on San Juan Hill and became the national hero of the war. As Governor of New York only months afterward, T.R. sponsored so many reform measures that he was promoted upstairs by standpat Republican bosses to run for Vice President on the ticket headed by William McKinley (whom Roosevelt once described as having the backbone of a chocolate éclair). After McKinley's assassination, he took the oath of office on September 14, 1901—at 42, the youngest President of the U.S. "My ambition," he wrote a friend, "is that, in however small a way, the work I do shall be along the Washington and Lincoln lines."

In domestic affairs, he launched the first successful antitrust suit ever brought by an American President to dissolve a corporate monopoly (the Northern Securities Co.) to safeguard the right of fair competition. In the great anthracite coal strike, his was the first Presidential mediation to protect the public interest in a massive struggle between management and labor. T.R. galvanized press and public in successive drives for the U.S.'s first pure food bill, the right for the Interstate Commerce Commission to regulate fair railroad rates.

In international affairs, T.R. was the first U.S. President to win the Nobel Peace Prize, for his brilliant negotiation of a conclusion to the Russo-Japanese War. He deterred Germany's rampaging Kaiser Wilhelm II from adventures in Venezuela and Morocco and helped hold off the outbreak of World War I. He dug the Panama Canal. In what he considered his greatest service to peace, he sent 16 battleships, all painted white—"the Great White Fleet"—on a year-long, good-will mission around the world. This was the American assurance that the American Dream might be global, and was surely here to stay.

In his personal conduct in the White House T.R.'s example was as significant as his accomplishments. The White House is a "bully pulpit," he said, and he was forever heckling, hectoring, encouraging his fellow citizens to lead more fruitful lives. "When I see a husky man going along with his wife, letting her carry the baby, I know that sort of fellow is no good," said the President. The White House was an arena of family romps and pillow fights, Presidential boxing and judo matches, crag-climbing excursions with foreign diplomats in Rock Creek Park, "the strenuous life" also of verse, biography and natural history. "Theodore . . . is drunk with himself," said one friend, Henry Adams, and another, Edith Wharton, thought the President lived each moment so intensely and so entirely that each encounter glowed like radium. A third, Oscar Straus, summed up, "He had the quality of vitalizing things," and as T.R. stepped down in favor of his friend William Howard Taft, the U.S.'s morale was soaring to the stars.

On January 6, 1919, after a doomed, third-party, Bull Moose run for the Presidency in 1912, and after passionate advocacy of U.S. entry into World War I, T.R. died, aged 60. "Both life and death are part of the same Great Adventure," said the unforgettable President Theodore Roosevelt.

How We Made the First Flight

by Orville Wright

Orville Wright, younger brother of Wilbur, had the honor of being at the controls on December 17, 1903, when their power-driven, heavier-than-air machine flew that first historic flight at Kitty Hawk, North Carolina.

The brothers, interested in mechanical devices from childhood, built bicycles as young adults. They became interested in the problems of flight in 1896 when they heard of the death of pioneer glider Otto Lilienthal. They eventually built their own gliders and flew them at Kitty Hawk because of the consistent, strong winds there.

In the following selection, Orville Wright describes the events that led up to the first flight in a heavier-than-air machine. He discusses he and Wilbur's need to build their own engine, their work on propellers, the repairs necessary for success, Wilbur's initial attempt on December 14, and the four successful flights on December 17.

The flights of the 1902 glider had demonstrated the efficiency of our system for maintaining equilibrium, and also the accuracy of the laboratory work upon which the design of the glider was based. We then felt that we were prepared to calculate in advance the performance of machines with a degree of accuracy that had never been possible with the data and tables possessed by our predecessors. Before leaving camp in 1902 we were already at work on the general design of a new machine which we proposed to propel with a motor.

Orville Wright, "How We Made the First Flight," Aviation Education Clearinghouse of the Federal Aviation Administration, www.aero-web.org.

Designing the Machine, Its Motor, and Propellers

Immediately upon our return to Dayton, we wrote to a number of automobile and motor builders, stating the purpose for which we desired a motor, and asking whether they could furnish one that would develop eight-brake horse power, with a weight complete not exceeding 200 pounds. Most of the companies answered that they were too busy with their regular business to undertake the building of such a motor for us. . . .

Finally we decided to undertake the building of the motor ourselves. We estimated that we could make one of four cylinders with 4 inch bore and 4 inch stroke, weighing not over two hundred pounds, including all accessories. . . .

Wilbur and I were busy in completing the design of the machine itself. The preliminary tests of the motor having convinced us that more than 8 horse power would be secured, we felt free to add enough weight to build a more substantial machine than we had originally contemplated.

Our tables of air pressures and our experience in flying with the 1902 glider enabled us, we thought, to calculate exactly the thrust necessary to sustain the machine in flight. But to design a propeller that would give this thrust with the power we had at our command, was a matter we had not as yet seriously considered. No data on air propellers was available, but we had always understood that it was not a difficult matter to secure an efficiency of 50% with marine propellers. All that would be necessary would be to learn the theory of the operation of marine propellers from books on marine engineering, and then substitute air pressures for water pressures. Accordingly we secured several such books from the Dayton Public Library. Much to our surprise, all the formulae on propellers contained in these books were of an empirical nature. There was no way of adapting them to calculations of aerial propellers. As we could afford neither the time nor expense of a long series of experiments to find by trial a propeller suitable for our machine, we decided to rely more on theory than was the practice with marine engineers.

It was apparent that a propeller was simply an aeroplane travelling in a spiral course. As we could calculate the effect of an aeroplane travelling in a straight course, why should we not be able to calculate the effect of one travelling in a spiral course? . . .

Our minds became so obsessed with it that we could do little other work. We engaged in innumerable discussions, and often after an hour or so of heated argument, we would discover that we were as far from agreement as when we started, but that both had changed to the other's original position in the discussion. After a couple of months of this study and discussion, we were able to follow the various reactions in their intricate relations long enough to begin to understand them. We realized that the thrust generated by a propeller when standing stationary was no indication of the thrust when in motion. The only way to really test the efficiency of propeller would be to actually try it on the machine.

For two reasons we decided to use two propellers. In the first place we could, by the use of two propellers, secure a reaction against a greater quantity of air, and at the same time use a larger pitch angle than was possible with one propeller; and in the second place by having the propellers turn in opposite direction, the gyroscopic action of one would neutralize that of the other. The method we adopted of driving the propellers in opposite directions by means of chains is now too well known to need description here. We decided to place the motor to one side of the man, so that in case of a plunge head first, the motor could not fall upon him. In our gliding experiments we had had a number of experiences in which we had landed upon one wing, but the crushing of the wing had absorbed the shock, so that we were not uneasy about the motor in case of a landing of that kind. To provide against the machine rolling over forward in landing, we designed skids like sled runners, extending out in front of the main surfaces. Otherwise the general construction and operation of the machine was to be similar to that of the 1902 glider. . . .

At Kitty Hawk

We left Dayton, September 23, and arrived at our camp at Kill Devil Hill on Friday, the 25th. We found there provisions and tools, which had been shipped by freight several weeks in advance. . . .

The next three weeks were spent in setting the motor-machine together. On days with more favourable winds we gained additional experience in handling a flyer by gliding with the 1902 machine, which we had found in pretty fair condition in the old building, where we had left it the year before. . . .

Just as the machine was ready for test, bad weather set in. It had been disagreeably cold for several weeks, so cold that we could scarcely work on the machine some days. But now we began to have rain and snow, and a wind of 25 to 30 miles blew for several days from the north. . . .

Monday, December 14th, was a beautiful day, but there was not enough wind to enable a start to be made from the level ground about camp. We therefore decided to attempt a flight from the side of the big Kill Devil Hill. We had arranged with the members of the Kill Devil Life Saving Station, which was located a little over a mile from our camp, to inform them when we were ready to make the first trial of the machine. We were soon joined by J.T. Daniels, Robert Westcott, Thomas Beacham, W.S. Dough and Uncle Benny O'Neal, of the Station, who helped us get the machine to the hill, a quarter mile away. We laid the track 150 feet up the side of the hill on a 9 degree slope. With the slope of the track, the thrust of the propellers and the machine starting directly into the wind, we did not anticipate any trouble in getting up flying speed on the 60 foot monorail track. But we did not feel certain the operator could keep the machine balanced on the track.

When the machine had been fastened with a wire to the track, so that it could not start until released by the operator, and the motor had been run to make sure that it was in condition, we tossed a coin to decide who should have the first trial. Wilbur won. I took a position at one of the wings intending to help balance the machine as it ran down the rack. But when the restraining wire was slipped, the machine started off so quickly I could stay with it only a few feet. After a 35- to 40-foot run, it lifted from the rail. But it was allowed to turn up too much. It climbed a few feet, stalled, and then settled to the ground near the foot of the hill, 105 feet below. My stop watch showed that I had been in the air just 3½ seconds. In landing the left wing touched first. The machine swung around, dug the skids into the sand and broke one of them. Several other parts were also broken, but the damage to the machine was not serious. While the test had shown nothing as to whether the power of the motor was sufficient to keep the machine up, since the landing was made many feet below the starting point, the experiment had demonstrated that the method adopted for launching the machine was a safe and practical one. On the whole, we were much pleased.

Two days were consumed in making repairs, and the machine was not ready again till late in the afternoon of the 16th. . . .

December 17

During the night of December 16, 1903, a strong cold wind blew from the north. When we arose on the morning of the 17th, the puddles of water, which had been standing about the camp since the recent rains, were covered with ice. The wind had a velocity of 10 to 12 meters per second (22 to 27 miles an hour). We thought it would die down before long, and so remained indoors the early part of the morning. But when ten o'clock arrived, and the wind was as brisk as ever, we decided that we had better get the machine out and attempt a flight. We hung out the signal for the men of the Life Saving Station. We thought that by facing the flyer into a strong wind, there ought to be no trouble in launching it from the level ground about camp. We realized the difficulties of flying in so high a wind, but estimated that the added dangers in flight would be partly compensated for by the slower speed in landing.

We laid the track on a smooth stretch of ground about one hundred feet north of the new building. The biting cold wind made work difficult, and we had to warm up frequently in our living room, where we had a good fire in an improvised stove made of a large carbide can. By the time all was ready, J.T. Daniels, W.S. Dough and A.D. Etheridge, members of the Kill Devil Life Saving Station; W.C. Brinkley of Manteo, and Johnny Moore, a boy from Nags Head, had arrived.

On December 17, 1903, the Wright brothers flew their aircraft, marking the first heavier-than-air flight in history.

We had a "Richard" hand anemometer with which we measured the velocity of the wind. Measurements made just before starting the first flight showed velocities of 11 to 12 meters per second, or 24 to 27 miles per hour. . . .

With all the knowledge and skill acquired in thousands of flights in the last ten years, I would hardly think today of making my first flight on a strange machine in a twenty-seven mile wind, even if I knew that the machine had already been flown and was safe. After these years of experience I look with amazement upon our audacity in attempting flights with a new and untried machine under such circumstances. Yet faith in our calculations and the design of the first machine, based upon our tables of air pressures, secured by months of careful laboratory work, and confidence in our system of control developed by three years of actual experiences in balancing gliders in the air had convinced us that the machine was capable of lifting and maintaining itself in the air, and that, with a little practice, it could be safely flown.

Wilbur, having used his turn in the unsuccessful attempt on the 14th, the right to the first trial now belonged to me. After running the motor a few minutes to heat it up, I released the wire that held the machine to the track, and the machine started forward in the wind. Wilbur ran at the side of the machine, holding the wing to balance it on the track. Unlike the start on the 14th, made in a calm, the machine, facing a 27-mile wind, started very slowly. Wilbur was able to stay with it till it lifted from the track after a forty-foot run. One of the Life Saving men snapped the camera for us, taking a picture just as the machine had reached the end of the track and had risen to a height of about two feet. The slow forward speed of the machine over the ground is clearly shown in the picture by Wilbur's attitude. He stayed along beside the machine without any effort.

The course of the flight up and down was exceedingly erratic, partly due to the irregularity of the air, and partly to lack of experience in handling this machine. The control of the front rudder was difficult on account of its being balanced too near the center. This gave it a tendency to turn itself when started; so that it turned too far on one side and then too far on the other. As a result the machine would rise suddenly to about ten feet, and then as suddenly dart for the ground. A sudden dart when a little over a hundred feet from the end of the track, or a little over 120 feet from the point at which it rose into the air, ended the flight. As the velocity of the wind was over 35 feet per second and the speed of the machine over the ground against this wind ten feet per second, the speed of the machine relative to the air was over 45 feet per second, and the length of the flight was equivalent to a flight of 540 feet made in calm air. This flight lasted only 12 seconds, but it was nevertheless the first in the history of the world in which a machine carrying a man had raised itself by its own power into the air in full flight, had sailed forward without reduction of speed and had finally landed at a point as high as that from which it started. . . .

At twenty minutes after eleven Wilbur started on the second flight. The course of this flight was much like that of the first, very much up and down. The speed over the ground was somewhat faster than that of the first flight, due to the lesser wind. The duration of the flight was less than a second longer than the first, but the distance covered was about seventy-five feet greater.

Twenty minutes later the third flight started. This one was steadier than the first one an hour before. I was proceeding along pretty well when a sudden gust from the right lifted the machine up twelve to fifteen feet and turned it up sidewise in an alarming manner. It began a lively sidling off to the left. I warped the wings to try to recover the lateral balance and at the same time pointed the machine down to reach the ground as quickly as possible. The lateral control was more effective than I had imagined and before I reached the ground the right wing was lower than the left and struck first. The time of this flight was fifteen seconds and the distance over the ground a little over 200 feet.

Wilbur started the fourth and last flight at just 12 o'clock. The first few hundred feet were up and down, as before, but by the time three hundred feet had been covered, the machine was under much better control. The course of the next four or five hundred feet had but little undulation. However, when out about eight hundred feet the machine began pitching again, and, in one of its darts downward, struck the ground. The distance over the ground was measured and found to be 852 feet; the time of the flight 59 seconds. The frame supporting the front rudder was badly broken, but the main part of the machine was not injured at all. We estimated that the machine could be put in condition for flight again in a day or two.

While we were standing about discussing this last flight, a sudden strong gust of wind struck the machine and began to turn it over. Everybody made a rush for it. Wilbur, who was at one end, seized it in front, Mr. Daniels and I, who were behind, tried to stop it by holding to the rear uprights. All our efforts were in vain. The machine rolled over and over. Daniels, who had retained his grip, was carried along with it, and was thrown about head over heels inside of the machine. Fortunately he was not seriously injured, though badly bruised in falling about against the motor, chain guides, etc. The ribs in the surface of the machine were broken, the motor injured and the chain guides badly bent, so that all possibility of further flights with it for that year were at an end.

4 The Wright Brothers Fly the First Heavier-than-Air Craft: December 17, 1903

The Flight of the Wright Brothers Changed the World

by Bill Gates

To mark the end of the twentieth century, *Time* used its website to profile one hundred individuals who shaped the last one hundred years. Bill Gates, chairman and CEO of computer software giant Microsoft, wrote a tribute to the Wright brothers, Wilbur and Orville, for the way their invention gave the world a tool for good and evil, created a cultural force, and made the world a smaller place.

W ilbur and Orville Wright were two brothers from the heartland of America with a vision as sweeping as the sky and a practicality as down-to-earth as the Wright Cycle Co., the bicycle business they founded in Dayton, Ohio, in 1892. But while there were countless bicycle shops in turn-of-the-century America, in only one were wings being built as well as wheels. When the Wright brothers finally realized their vision of powered human flight in 1903, they made the world a forever smaller place. I've been to Kitty Hawk, N.C., and seen where the brothers imagined the future, and then literally flew across its high frontier. It was an inspiration to be there, and to soak up the amazing perseverance and creativity of these two pioneers. . . .

The Wright brothers gave us a tool, but it was up to individuals and nations to put it to use, and use it we have. The airplane revolutionized both peace and war. It brought families together: once, when a child or other close relatives left the old country for America, family and friends mourned for someone they would never see again. Today, the grandchild of that immigrant can return again and again across a vast ocean in just half a turn of the clock. But the airplane also helped tear families apart, by making international warfare an effortless reality.

The Wrights created one of the greatest cultural forces since the development of writing, for their invention effectively became the World Wide Web of that era, bringing people, languages, ideas and values together. It also ushered in an age of globalization, as the world's flight paths became the superhighways of an emerging international economy. Those superhighways of the sky not only revolutionized international business; they also opened up isolated economies, carried the cause of democracy around the world and broke down every kind of political barrier. And they set travelers on a path that would eventually lead beyond Earth's atmosphere.

The Wright brothers and their invention, then, sparked a revolution as far-reaching as the industrial and digital revolutions. But that revolution did not come about by luck or accident. It was vision, quiet resolve and the application of scientific methodology that enabled Orville and Wilbur to carry the human race skyward. Their example reminds us that genius doesn't have a pedigree, and that you don't discover new worlds by plying safe, conventional waters. With 10 years of hindsight, even Orville Wright admitted that "I look with amazement upon our audacity in attempting flights with a new and untried machine.". . .

We have to understand that engineering breakthroughs are not just mechanical or scientific—they are liberating forces that can continually improve people's lives. Who would have thought, as the 20th century opened, that one of its greatest contributions would come from two obscure, fresh-faced young Americans who pursued the utmost bounds of human thought and gave us all, for the first time, the power literally to sail beyond the sunset.

The 20th century has been the American Century in large part because of great inventors such as the Wright brothers. May we follow their flight paths and blaze our own in the 21st century.

Henry Ford Establishes a Car Manufacturing Company: 1903

Ford Creates New Ways to Make and Sell Cars

by Henry Ford with Samuel Crowther

Henry Ford became a legend in business when he started his own car company. He built the Model T, the first affordable car for the common person, and he pioneered assembly-line production techniques that drove down the price of his cars.

In the selection that follows, Ford talks about the formative years of the car company that still bears his name. He discusses his first success, the Model A—its longevity and the ads he used to sell it. Later, he tells of building the famous Model T. Finally, he covers the principles behind his successful use of the assembly line to mass produce a cheap car for the masses.

Coauthor Samuel Crowther wrote many books on the industrial age in America. Some of his titles include *The Presidency vs. Hoover, Prohibition and Prosperity*, and another book with Henry Ford, *My Friend Mr. Edison*.

The original company and its equipment, as may be gathered, were not elaborate. We rented Strelow's carpenter shop on Mack Avenue. In making my designs I had also worked out the methods of making, but, since at that time we could not afford to buy machinery, the entire car was made according to my designs, but by various manufacturers, and about all we did, even in the way of assembling, was to put on the wheels, the tires, and

---

Henry Ford with Samuel Crowther, *My Life and Work*. New York: Doubleday, Page & Company, 1922.

the body. That would really be the most economical method of manufacturing if only one could be certain that all of the various parts would be made on the manufacturing plan that I have above outlined. The most economical manufacturing of the future will be that in which the whole of an article is not made under one roof—unless, of course, it be a very simple article. The modern—or better, the future—method is to have each part made where it may best be made and then assemble the parts into a complete unit at the points of consumption. That is the method we are now following and expect to extend. . . .

I had been experimenting principally upon the cutting down of weight. Excess weight kills any self-propelled vehicle. There are a lot of fool ideas about weight. . . . Whenever any one suggests to me that I might increase weight or add a part, I look into decreasing weight and eliminating a part! The car that I designed was lighter than any car that had yet been made. It would have been lighter if I had known how to make it so—later I got the materials to make the lighter car.

In our first year we built "Model A," selling the runabout for eight hundred and fifty dollars and the tonneau for one hundred dollars more. This model had a two-cylinder opposed motor developing eight horsepower. It had a chain drive, a seventy-two inch wheel base—which was supposed to be long—and a fuel capacity of five gallons. We made and sold 1,708 cars in the first year. That is how well the public responded.

Every one of these "Model A's" has a history. Take No. 420. Colonel D.C. Collier of California bought it in 1904. He used it for a couple of years, sold it, and bought a new Ford. No. 420 changed hands frequently until 1907 when it was bought by one Edmund Jacobs living near Ramona in the heart of the mountains. He drove it for several years in the roughest kind of work. Then he bought a new Ford and sold his old one. By 1915 No. 420 had passed into the hands of a man named Cantello who took out the motor, hitched it to a water pump, rigged up shafts on the chassis and now, while the motor chugs away at the pumping of water, the chassis drawn by a burro acts as a buggy. The moral, of course, is that you can dissect a Ford but you cannot kill it.

In our first advertisement we said:

Our purpose is to construct and market an automobile specially designed for everyday wear and tear—business, professional, and family use; an automobile which will attain to a sufficient speed to

satisfy the average person without acquiring any of those break-
neck velocities which are so universally condemned; a machine
which will be admired by man, woman, and child alike for its com-
pactness, its simplicity, its safety, its all-around convenience, and—
last but not least—its exceedingly reasonable price, which places
it within the reach of many thousands who could not think of paying the comparatively fabulous prices asked for most machines.

And these are the points we emphasized:
Good material.
Simplicity—most of the cars at that time required consider-
able skill in their management.
The engine.
The ignition—which was furnished by two sets of six dry cell
batteries.
The automatic oiling.
The simplicity and the ease of control of the transmission,
which was of the planetary type.
The workmanship.
We did not make the pleasure appeal. We never have. In its first
advertising we showed that a motor car was a utility. We said:

We often hear quoted the old proverb, "Time is money"—and yet
how few business and professional men act as if they really believed its truth.

Men who are constantly complaining of shortage of time and
lamenting the fewness of days in the week—men to whom every
five minutes wasted means a dollar thrown away—men to whom
five minutes' delay sometimes means the loss of many dollars—
will yet depend on the haphazard, uncomfortable, and limited
means of transportation afforded by street cars, etc., when the in-
vestment of an exceedingly moderate sum in the purchase of a per-
fected, efficient, high-grade automobile would cut out anxiety and
unpunctuality and provide a luxurious means of travel ever at your
beck and call.

Always ready, always sure.

Built to save you time and consequent money.

Built to take you anywhere you want to go and bring you back
again on time.

Built to add to your reputation for punctuality; to keep your customers good-humoured and in a buying mood.

Built for business or pleasure—just as you say.

Built also for the good of your health—to carry you "jarlessly" over any kind of half decent roads, to refresh your brain with the luxury of much "out-doorness" and your lungs with the "tonic of tonics"—the right kind of atmosphere.

It is your say, too, when it comes to speed. You can—if you choose—loiter lingeringly through shady avenues or you can press down on the foot-lever until all the scenery looks alike to you and you have to keep your eyes skinned to count the milestones as they pass.

I am giving the gist of this advertisement to show that, from the beginning, we were looking to providing service—we never bothered with a "sporting car."

The business went along almost as by magic. The cars gained a reputation for standing up. They were tough, they were simple, and they were well made. I was working on my design for a universal single model but I had not settled the designs nor had we the money to build and equip the proper kind of plant for manufacturing. . . .

My associates were not convinced that it was possible to restrict our cars to a single model. The automobile trade was following the old bicycle trade, in which every manufacturer thought it necessary to bring out a new model each year and to make it so unlike all previous models that those who had bought the former models would want to get rid of the old and buy the new. That was supposed to be good business. . . . The plan which I then had in the back of my head but to which we were not then sufficiently advanced to give expression, was that, when a model was settled upon then every improvement on that model should be interchangeable with the old model, so that a car should never get out of date. It is my ambition to have every piece of machinery, or other non-consumable product that I turn out, so strong and so well made that no one ought ever to have to buy a second one. A good machine of any kind ought to last as long as a good watch. . . .

The Model T

Therefore in 1909 I announced one morning, without any previous warning, that in the future we were going to build only one

Ford revolutionized automobile production. Fresh from the assembly line, a Model T's engine is started.

model, that the model was going to be "Model T," and that the chassis would be exactly the same for all cars, and I remarked:

"Any customer can have a car painted any colour that he wants so long as it is black."

I cannot say that any one agreed with me. The selling people could not of course see the advantages that a single model would bring about in production. More than that, they did not particularly care. They thought that our production was good enough as it was and there was a very decided opinion that lowering the sales price would hurt sales, that the people who wanted quality would be driven away and that there would be none to replace them. There was very little conception of the motor industry. A motor car was still regarded as something in the way of a luxury. The manufacturers did a good deal to spread this idea. Some clever persons invented the name "pleasure car" and the advertising emphasized the pleasure features. The sales people had ground for their objections and particularly when I made the following announcement:

I will build a motor car for the great multitude. It will be large enough for the family but small enough for the individual to run and care for. It will be constructed of the best materials, by the best men to be hired, after the simplest designs that modern engineering can devise. But it will be so low in price that no man making a good salary will be unable to own one—and enjoy with his family the blessing of hours of pleasure in God's great open spaces.

This announcement was received not without pleasure. The general comment was:
"If Ford does that he will be out of business in six months.". . .

Production Ideas

The more economical methods of production did not begin all at once. They began gradually—just as we began gradually to make our own parts. "Model T" was the first motor that we made ourselves. The great economies began in assembling and then extended to other sections so that, while to-day we have skilled mechanics in plenty, they do not produce automobiles—they make it easy for others to produce them. Our skilled men are the tool makers, the experimental workmen, the machinists, and the pattern makers. They are as good as any men in the world—so good, indeed, that they should not be wasted in doing that which the machines they contrive can do better. The rank and file of men come to us unskilled; they learn their jobs within a few hours or a few days. . . .

A Ford car contains about five thousand parts—that is counting screws, nuts, and all. Some of the parts are fairly bulky and others are almost the size of watch parts. In our first assembling we simply started to put a car together at a spot on the floor and workmen brought to it the parts as they were needed in exactly the same way that one builds a house. When we started to make parts it was natural to create a single department of the factory to make that part, but usually one workman performed all of the operations necessary on a small part. The rapid press of production made it necessary to devise plans of production that would avoid having the workers falling over one another. The undirected worker spends more of his time walking about for materials and tools than he does in working; he gets small pay because pedestrianism is not a highly paid line.

The first step forward in assembly came when we began taking the work to the men instead of the men to the work. We now have two general principles in all operations—that a man shall never have to take more than one step, if possibly it can be avoided, and that no man need ever stoop over.

The principles of assembly are these:

(1) Place the tools and the men in the sequence of the operation so that each component part shall travel the least possible distance while in the process of finishing.

(2) Use work slides or some other form of carrier so that when a workman completes his operation, he drops the part always in the same place—which place must always be the most convenient place to his hand—and if possible have gravity carry the part to the next workman for his operation.

(3) Use sliding assembling lines by which the parts to be assembled are delivered at convenient distances.

The net result of the application of these principles is the reduction of the necessity for thought on the part of the worker and the reduction of his movements to a minimum. He does as nearly as possible only one thing with only one movement. . . .

The Assembly Line

Along about April 1, 1913, we first tried the experiment of an assembly line. We tried it on assembling the fly-wheel magneto. We try everything in a little way first—we will rip out anything once we discover a better way, but we have to know absolutely that the new way is going to be better than the old before we do anything drastic.

I believe that this was the first moving line ever installed. The idea came in a general way from the overhead trolley that the Chicago packers use in dressing beef. We had previously assembled the fly-wheel magneto in the usual method. With one workman doing a complete job he could turn out from thirty-five to forty pieces in a nine-hour day, or about twenty minutes to an assembly. What he did alone was then spread into twenty-nine operations; that cut down the assembly time to thirteen minutes, ten seconds. Then we raised the height of the line eight inches—this was in 1914—and cut the time to seven minutes. Further experimenting with the speed that the work should move at cut the time down to five minutes. In short, the result is this: by the aid of scientific study one man is now able to do somewhat more than four did only a comparatively few years ago. That line established the efficiency of the method and we now use it everywhere. The assembling of the motor, formerly done by one man, is now divided into eighty-four operations—those men do the work that three times their number formerly did. In a short time we tried out the plan on the chassis.

About the best we had done in stationary chassis assembling was an average of twelve hours and twenty-eight minutes per chassis. We tried the experiment of drawing the chassis with a rope and windlass down a line two hundred fifty feet long. Six assemblers travelled with the chassis and picked up the parts from piles placed along the line. This rough experiment reduced the time to five hours fifty minutes per chassis. In the early part of 1914 we elevated the assembly line. We had adopted the policy of "man-high" work; we had one line twenty-six and three quarter inches and another twenty-four and one half inches from the floor—to suit squads of different heights. The waist-high arrangement and a further subdivision of work so that each man had fewer movements cut down the labour time per chassis to one hour thirty-three minutes. Only the chassis was then assembled in the line. . . .

It must not be imagined, however, that all this worked out as quickly as it sounds. The speed of the moving work had to be carefully tried out; in the fly-wheel magneto we first had a speed of sixty inches per minute. That was too fast. Then we tried eighteen inches per minute. That was too slow. Finally we settled on forty-four inches per minute. The idea is that a man must not be hurried in his work—he must have every second necessary but not a single unnecessary second. We have worked out speeds for each assembly, for the success of the chassis assembly caused us gradually to overhaul our entire method of manufacturing and to put all assembling in mechanically driven lines. The chassis assembling line, for instance, goes at a pace of six feet per minute; the front axle assembly line goes at one hundred eighty-nine inches per minute. In the chassis assembling are forty-five separate operations or stations. The first men fasten four mud-guard brackets to the chassis frame; the motor arrives on the tenth operation and so on in detail. Some men do only one or two small operations, others do more. The man who places a part does not fasten it—the part may not be fully in place until after several operations later. The man who puts in a bolt does not put on the nut; the man who puts on the nut does not tighten it. . . .

Essentially the same ideas have been applied to the assembling of the motor. In October, 1913, it required nine hours and fifty-four minutes of labour time to assemble one motor; six months later, by the moving assembly method, this time had been reduced to five hours and fifty-six minutes. Every piece of work in the shops moves; it may move on hooks on overhead chains going to assembly in the exact order in which the parts are required; it may travel on a moving platform, or it may go by gravity, but the point is that there is no lifting or trucking of anything other than materials. . . .

Dividing and subdividing operations, keeping the work in motion—those are the keynotes of production. But also it is to be remembered that all the parts are designed so that they can be most easily made. And the saving? Although the comparison is not quite fair, it is startling. If at our present rate of production we employed the same number of men per car that we did when we began in 1903—and those men were only for assembly—we should to-day require a force of more than two hundred thousand. We have less than fifty thousand men on automobile production at our highest point of around four thousand cars a day!

Albert Einstein's Remarkable Year Changes How the World Perceives the Universe

by Robert B. Downs

With his droopy moustache and his wild tangle of white hair, Albert Einstein was one of the most recognized scientists of the twentieth century. But it was the work he completed in his twenties that revolutionized scientific thought. One particular year, 1905, saw him produce his greatest contributions to knowledge.

The selection below was written by Robert B. Downs, a former president of the American Library Association and Dean of Library Administration at the University of Illinois. Downs is an authority on and champion of intellectual freedom. He is editor of *The First Freedom*, a comprehensive anthology on literary censorship. In this passage he discusses the three major papers Einstein produced in 1905 dealing with relativity and the characteristics of light. He also explores the significance of these and other discoveries of Einstein.

Robert B. Downs, *Books That Changed the World*. New York: New American Library, 1956.

The Einstein revolution began in 1905, with the appearance in a German journal, *Annalen der Physik*, of a thirty-page paper carrying the unexciting title "On the Electrodynamics of Moving Bodies." At the time, Einstein was only twenty-six years of age, and serving as a minor official in the Swiss patent office. He had been born into a middle-class Jewish family at Ulm, Bavaria, in 1879. As a student, he was not precocious except in mathematics, a field in which he displayed early evidences of genius. Because of failure of the family fortune, Einstein was forced out on his own at fifteen. Emigrating to Switzerland, he was able to continue his scientific education at the Polytechnic Academy in Zurich, married a fellow student, and became a Swiss citizen. Denied his ambition for a university professorship, in order to earn a living he settled in a job making preliminary reports and rewriting inventors' applications for the patent office. His spare time was used for intensive study of the works of philosophers, scientists, and mathematicians. Soon he was ready to launch the first of a flood of original contributions to science, destined to have far-ranging repercussions.

Einstein and Relativity

In his 1905 paper, Einstein set forth the Special Theory of Relativity, challenging man's existing concepts of time and space, of matter and energy. The foundations for the theory were laid down in two basic assumptions. The first was the principle of relativity: all motion is relative. A familiar illustration of the principle is a moving train or ship. A person sitting in a train with darkened windows would have, if there was little commotion, no idea of speed or direction, or perhaps even that the train was moving at all. A man on a ship with portholes closed would be in a similar predicament. We conceive motion only in relative terms, that is in respect to other objects. On a vastly greater scale, the forward movement of the earth could not be detected if there were no heavenly bodies for comparisons.

Einstein's second major hypothesis was that the velocity of light is independent of the motion of its source. The speed of light, 186,000 miles a second, is always the same, anywhere in the universe, regardless of place, time or direction. Light travels in a moving train, for instance, at exactly the same speed as it does outside the train. No force can make it go faster or slower. Furthermore, nothing can exceed the velocity of light, though electrons closely approximate it. Light is, in fact, the only constant, unvarying factor in all of nature.

A famous experiment carried out by two American scientists, Michelson and Morley, in 1887, furnished the basis for Einstein's theory on light. To measure the speed of light with absolute exactness, an ingenious apparatus was built. Two pipes, each a mile in length, were placed at right angles to each other. One pipe was pointed in the direction of the earth's journey around the sun, and the second against the direction of the earth's motion. At the end of each pipe a mirror was placed and a beam of light shot into both pipes at exactly the same instant. If the theory then prevailing was true, that an invisible ether filled all space not occupied by solid objects, one ray of light would have been analogous to a swimmer crossing against the current, while the other was comparable to a swimmer going down stream. To the astonishment and mystification of the scientists, however, the two beams of light came back together, at the same identical moment. The experiment was considered a failure.

Einstein's paper in 1905 answered the question which had puzzled Michelson, Morley, and their fellow physicists. The existence of ether was rejected, and the experiment with the pipes had actually measured the speed of light correctly. The essential point deduced by Einstein was that light always travels at the same velocity no matter under what conditions it is measured, and the motion of the earth in regard to the sun has no influence upon the speed of light.

Differing with Newton's teachings, Einstein asserted that there is no such thing as absolute motion. The idea of absolute motion of a body in space is meaningless. Every body's movement is relative to that of another. Motion is the natural state of all things. Nowhere on earth or in the universe is there anything absolutely at rest. Throughout our restless cosmos, movement is constant, from the infinitesimally small atom to the largest celestial galaxies. For example, the earth is moving around the sun at the rate of twenty miles a second. In a universe where all is motion and fixed points of reference are lacking, there are no established standards for comparing velocities, length, size, mass, and time, except as they might be measured by relative motions. Only light is not relative, its velocity remaining changeless regardless of its source or the observer's position, as the Michelson-Morley experiment demonstrated.

Relativity of Time

Doubtless the most difficult of all Einsteinian concepts to comprehend and the most unsettling to traditional beliefs is the relativity of time. Einstein held that events at different places occurring at the same moment for one observer do not occur at the same moment for another observer moving relatively to the first. For example, two events judged as taking place at the same time by an observer on the ground are not simultaneous for an observer in a train or an airplane. Time is relative to the position and speed of the observer, and is not absolute. Applying the theory to the universe, an event on a distant star, say an explosion, witnessed by an earth dweller, did not occur on the star at the same time as it was seen on the earth. On the contrary, though light moves at 186,000 miles a second, an occurrence on a remote star may have taken place years before news of it reached our world. The star seen today is actually the star as it appeared long ago. Conceivably it may have even ceased to exist.

If it were possible to conceive of a human being attaining speed greater than the velocity of light, according to the theory of relativity, he could overtake his past and his birth would occur in the future. Every moving planet has its own system of time, varying from time schedules found elsewhere. A day on our planet is merely the period required for the earth to rotate on its axis. Since Jupiter takes more time in its revolution around the sun than does the earth, a year on Jupiter is longer than the earth's year. As speed increases, time slows down. We are accustomed to the thought that every physical object has three dimensions, but time, maintains Einstein, is also a dimension of space, and space is a dimension of time. Neither time nor space can exist without the other and they are, therefore, interdependent. Because movement and change are constant, we live in a four-dimensional universe, with time as the fourth dimension.

Thus the two basic premises of Einstein's theory, as first presented a half-century ago, were the relativity of all motions and the concept of light as the only unvarying quantity in the universe.

In developing the principle of relativity of motion, Einstein upset another firmly established belief. Previously, length and mass had been regarded as absolute and constant under every conceivable circumstance. Now, Einstein came along to state that the mass or weight of an object and its length depend on how fast the body is moving. As an example, he imagined a train one thousand feet long, traveling at four-fifths of the speed of light. To a stationary observer, watching it pass by, the length of the train would be reduced to only six hundred feet, though it would remain a thousand feet to a passenger on the train. Similarly, any material body traveling through space contracts according to velocity. A yardstick, if it could be shot through space at 161,000 miles per second would shrink to a half-yard. The rotation of the earth has the curious effect of diminishing its circumference by about three inches.

Mass, too is changeable. As velocity increases, the mass of an object becomes greater. Experiments have shown that particles of matter speeded up to eighty-six per cent of the speed of light weigh twice as much as they do when at rest. That fact had tremendous implications for the development of atomic energy.

Einstein's original statement of 1905 is known as the Special Theory of Relativity because its conclusions are limited to uniform motion in a straight line, and are not concerned with other kinds of motion. In our cosmos, however, stars, planets, and other celestial bodies seldom move uniformly in a straight line. Any theory, therefore, which fails to include every type of motion offers an incomplete description of the universe. Einstein's next step, accordingly, was the formulation of his General Theory of Relativity, a process which required ten years of intensive application. In the General Theory, Einstein studied the mysterious force that guides the movements of the stars, comets, meteors, galaxies, and other bodies whirling around in the vast universe.

Einstein's Later Theory

In his General Theory of Relativity, published in 1915, Einstein advanced a new concept of gravitation, making fundamental changes in the ideas of gravity and light which had been generally accepted since the time of Sir Isaac Newton. Gravity had been regarded by Newton as a "force." Einstein proved, however, that the space around a planet or other celestial body is a gravitational field similar to the magnetic field around a magnet. Tremendous bodies, such as the sun or stars, are surrounded by enormous gravitational fields. The earth's attraction for the moon is thus explained. The theory also explained the erratic movements of Mercury, the planet nearest the sun, a phenomenon that had puzzled astronomers for centuries and had not been adequately covered by Newton's law of gravitation. So powerful are the great gravitational fields that they even bend rays of light. In 1919, a few years after the General Theory was first announced, photographs taken of a complete eclipse of the sun conclusively demonstrated the validity of Einstein's theory that light rays passing through the sun's gravitational field travel in curves rather than in straight lines.

There followed from this premise a statement by Einstein that space is curved. Revolving planets follow the shortest possible routes, influenced by the sun's presence, just as a river flowing toward the sea follows the contour of the land, along the easiest and most natural course. In our terrestrial scheme of things, a ship or airplane crossing the ocean follows a curved line, that is the arc of a circle, and not a straight line. It is evident, therefore, that the shortest distance between two points is a curve instead of a straight line. An identical rule governs the movements of a planet or light ray.

If Einstein's theory of curved space is accepted, a logical deduction is that space is finite. A light ray from a star, for example, eventually returns, after hundreds of millions of years, to the point from which it emanated, like a traveler who circumnavigates the earth. The universe does not extend forever into space, but has finite limitations, though no definite boundaries can be established.

The Effects of His Theories

Of all the great scientific discoveries and findings coming from Einstein, his contributions to atomic theory have had the most direct and profound effect on the present-day world. Shortly after his first paper on relativity was published in 1905, in the *Annalen der Physik*, the same journal carried a short article by Einstein projecting his theory further. It was entitled "Does the Inertia of a Body Depend on Its Energy?" The use of atomic energy, declared Einstein, is possible—at least in principle. The release of this tremendous force could be achieved according to a formula which he offered, the most celebrated equation in history: $E = mc^2$. To interpret, energy equals mass multiplied by the speed of light and again by the speed of light. If all the energy in a half pound of any matter could be utilized, Einstein held, enough power would be released to equal the explosive force of seven million tons of TNT. Without Einstein's equation, as one commentator pointed out, "experimenters might still have stumbled upon the fission of uranium, but it is doubtful if they would have realized its significance in terms of energy, or of bombs."

In the famous equation $E = mc^2$, Einstein demonstrated that energy and mass are the same thing, differing only in state. Mass is actually concentrated energy. The formula, wrote [Lincoln] Barnett in a brilliant evaluation, "provides the answer to many of the long-standing mysteries of physics. It explains how radioactive substances like radium and uranium are able to eject particles at enormous velocities and to go on doing so for millions of years. It explains how the sun and all the stars can go on radiating light and heat for billions of years, for if our sun were being consumed by ordinary processes of combustion the earth would have died in frozen darkness eons ago. It reveals the magnitude of the energy that slumbers in the nuclei of atoms, and forecasts how many grams of uranium must go into a bomb in order to destroy a city."

Einstein's equation remained a theory until 1939. By that time, its author had become a resident, and was shortly to become a citizen, of the United States, for he had been driven out of Europe by the Nazis. Learning that the Germans were engaged in importing uranium and were carrying on research on an atomic bomb, Einstein wrote President Roosevelt a highly confidential letter:

> Some recent work by E. Fermi and L. Szilard which has been communicated to me in manuscript, leads me to expect that the element uranium may be turned into a new and important source of energy in the immediate future. . . . This new phenomenon would also lead to the construction of bombs, and it is conceivable . . . that . . . a single bomb of this type, carried by boat and exploded in a port, might very well destroy the whole port together with some of the surrounding territory.

As an immediate result of Einstein's letter to Roosevelt, construction of the Manhattan atom-bomb project was started. About five years later, the first bomb was exploded at the Almagordo Reservation in New Mexico, and shortly thereafter the dreadful destruction caused by a bomb dropped on Hiroshima was instrumental in bringing the war with Japan to a quick end.

Though the atomic bomb was the most spectacular of all practical applications of Einstein's theories, his fame was also established by another remarkable accomplishment. Almost simultaneously with his Special Theory of Relativity in 1905, there was developed Einstein's Photoelectric Law, explaining the mysterious photoelectric effect, paving the way for the coming of television, motion-picture sound tracks, and the "electric eye," with its varied uses. It was for this discovery that Einstein was awarded the Nobel Prize in physics in 1922.

In his later years, Einstein labored indefatigably on what is known as the Unified Field Theory, attempting to demonstrate the harmony and uniformity of nature. According to his view, physical laws for the minute atom should be equally applicable to immense celestial bodies. The Unified Field Theory would unite all physical phenomena into a single scheme. Gravitation, electricity, magnetism, and atomic energy are all forces that would be covered by the one theory. In 1950, after more than a generation of research, Einstein presented such a theory to the world. He expressed the belief that the theory holds the key to the universe, unifying in one concept the infinitesimal, whirling world of the atom and the vast reaches of star-filled space. Because of mathematical difficulties, the theory has not yet been fully checked against established facts in physics. Einstein had unshaken faith, however, that his Unified Field Theory would in time produce an explanation of the "atomic character of energy," and demonstrate the existence of a well-ordered universe.

The philosophy which inspired and guided Einstein through decades of intense intellectual effort, and the rewards thereof, were described by him in a lecture on the origins of the General Theory of Relativity, at the University of Glasgow in 1933.

> The final results appear almost simple; any intelligent undergraduate can understand them without much trouble. But the years of searching in the dark for a truth that one feels, but cannot express; the intense desire and the alternations of confidence and misgiving, until one breaks through to clarity and understanding, are only known to him who has himself experienced them.

On another occasion, Einstein gave evidence of the deeply spiritual side of his nature by this statement:

> The most beautiful and most profound emotion we can experience is the sensation of the mystical. It is the sower of all true science. He to whom this emotion is a stranger, who can no longer wonder and stand rapt in awe, is as good as dead. To know that what is im-

penetrable to us really exists, manifesting itself as the highest wisdom and the most radiant beauty which our dull faculties can comprehend only in their most primitive forms—this knowledge, this feeling is at the center of true religiousness.

Innumerable scientists have paid tribute to Einstein. Quotations from two recent reviews of his career will illustrate his unique hold on the scientific world. Paul Oehser wrote:

Influence is a weak word for the work of Albert Einstein. The theories he advanced were revolutionary. In them was born the Atomic Age, and where it leads mankind we know not. But we do know that here is the greatest scientist and philosopher of our century, who has become almost a saint in our eyes and whose achievement is a justification of our faith in the human mind, a symbol of man's eternal quest, his reaching for the stars.

Another scientist, Banesh Hoffman, concluded:

The importance of Einstein's scientific ideas does not reside merely in their great success. Equally powerful has been their psychological effect. At a crucial epoch in the history of science Einstein demonstrated that long-accepted ideas were not in any way sacred. And it was this more than anything else that freed the imaginations of men like Bohr and de Broglie and inspired their daring triumphs in the realm of the quantum. Wherever we look, the physics of the 20th century bears the indelible imprint of Einstein's genius.

An Excerpt from *The Jungle*

by Upton Sinclair

Upton Sinclair started writing at the age of fifteen in order to pay his way through college. In 1906 he wrote *The Jungle*, which exposed the terrible conditions in the Chicago stockyards around the turn of the century. He was one of many "muckrakers" at this time, a word coined to describe writers who exposed various political or economic evils in American society. He went on to write critically about capitalism, coal mines, the press, higher education, and the oil industry. Some critics say that, of all American authors, Sinclair remains the most widely read abroad.

In the following selection, taken from *The Jungle*, Sinclair tells the story of Jurgis and Ona, two immigrants who come to Chicago, looking for a better life. He reveals terrible living conditions and brutal jobs that sap the strength and spirit of the two newcomers as they work in Packingtown, Sinclair's name for the stockyards.

Later that afternoon he and Ona went out to take a walk and look about them, to see more of this district which was to be their home. In back of the yards the dreary two-story frame houses were scattered farther apart, and there were great spaces bare—that seemingly had been overlooked by the great sore of a city as it spread itself over the surface of the prairie. These bare places were grown up with dingy, yellow weeds, hiding innumerable tomato cans; innumerable children played upon them, chasing one another here and there, screaming and fight-

Upton Sinclair, *The Jungle*. New York: The New American Library, 1960.

ing. The most uncanny thing about this neighborhood was the number of the children; you thought there must be a school just out, and it was only after long acquaintance that you were able to realize that there was no school, but that these were the children of the neighborhood—that there were so many children to the block in Packingtown that nowhere on its streets could a horse and buggy move faster than a walk!

It could not move faster anyhow, on account of the state of the streets. Those through which Jurgis and Ona were walking resembled streets less than they did a miniature topographical map. The roadway was commonly several feet lower than the level of the houses, which were sometimes joined by high boardwalks; there were no pavements—there were mountains and valleys and rivers, gullies and ditches, and great hollows full of stinking green water. In these pools the children played, and rolled about in the mud of the streets; here and there one noticed them digging in it, after trophies which they had stumbled on. One wondered about this, as also about the swarms of flies which hung about the scene, literally blackening the air, and the strange, fetid odor which assailed one's nostrils, a ghastly odor, of all the dead things of the universe. It impelled the visitor to questions—and then the residents would explain, quietly, that all this was "made" land, and that it had been "made" by using it as a dumping ground for the city garbage. After a few years the unpleasant effect of this would pass away, it was said; but meantime, in hot weather—and especially when it rained—the flies were apt to be annoying. Was it not unhealthful? the stranger would ask, and the residents would answer, "Perhaps; but there is no telling."

A little way further on, and Jurgis and Ona, staring open-eyed and wondering, came to the place where this "made" ground was in process of making. Here was a great hole, perhaps two city blocks square, and with long files of garbage wagons creeping into it. The place had an odor for which there are no polite words, and it was sprinkled over with children, who raked in it from dawn till dark. Sometimes visitors from the packing houses would wander out to see this "dump," and they would stand by and debate as to whether the children were eating the food they got, or merely collecting it for the chickens at home. Apparently none of them ever went down to find out.

Beyond this dump there stood a great brickyard, with smoking chimneys. First they took out the soil to make bricks, and

then they filled it up again with garbage, which seemed to Jurgis
and Ona a felicitous arrangement, characteristic of an enterpris-
ing country like America. A little way beyond was another great
hole, which they had emptied and not yet filled up. This held water, and all summer it stood there, with the nearby soil draining
into it, festering and stewing in the sun; and then, when winter
came, somebody cut the ice on it, and sold it to the people of the
city. This, too, seemed to the newcomers an economical arrangement; for they did not read the newspapers, and their heads were
not full of troublesome thoughts about "germs."

They stood there while the sun went down upon this scene,
and the sky in the west turned blood red, and the tops of the
houses shone like fire. Jurgis and Ona were not thinking of the
sunset, however—their backs were turned to it, and all their
thoughts were of Packingtown, which they could see so plainly
in the distance. The line of the buildings stood clear-cut and black
against the sky; here and there out of the mass rose the great
chimneys, with the river of smoke streaming away to the end of
the world. It was a study in colors now, this smoke; in the sunset
light it was black and brown and gray and purple. All the sordid
suggestions of the place were gone—in the twilight it was a vision of power. To the two who stood watching while the darkness
swallowed it up, it seemed a dream of wonder, with its tale of human energy, of things being done, of employment for thousands
upon thousands of men, of opportunity and freedom, of life and
love and joy. When they came away, arm in arm, Jurgis was saying, "Tomorrow I shall go there and get a job!" . . .

One curious thing [Jurgis] had noticed, the very first day, in
his profession of shoveler of guts; which was the sharp trick of
the floor bosses whenever there chanced to come a "slunk" calf.
Any man who knows anything about butchering knows that the
flesh of a cow that is about to calve, or has just calved, is not fit
for food. A good many of these came every day to the packing
houses—and, of course, if they had chosen, it would have been
an easy matter for the packers to keep them till they were fit for
food. But for the saving of time and fodder, it was the law that
cows of that sort came along with the others, and whoever noticed it would tell the boss, and the boss would start up a conversation with the government inspector, and the two would stroll
away. So in a trice the carcass of the cow would be cleaned out,
and the entrails would have vanished; it was Jurgis's task to slide

them into the trap, calves and all, and on the floor below they took out these "slunk" calves, and butchered them for meat, and used even the skins of them.

One day a man slipped and hurt his leg; and that afternoon, when the last of the cattle had been disposed of, and the men were leaving, Jurgis was ordered to remain and do some special work which this injured man had usually done. It was late, almost dark, and the government inspectors had all gone, and there were only a dozen or two of men on the floor. That day they had killed about four thousand cattle, and these cattle had come in freight trains from far states, and some of them had got hurt. There were some with broken legs, and some with gored sides; there were some that had died, from what cause no one could say; and they were all to be disposed of, here in darkness and silence. "Downers," the men called them; and the packing house had a special elevator upon which they were raised to the killing beds, where the gang proceeded to handle them, with an air of businesslike nonchalance which said plainer than any words that it was a matter of everyday routine. It took a couple of hours to get them out of the way, and in the end Jurgis saw them go into the chilling rooms with the rest of the meat, being carefully scattered here and there so that they could not be identified. When he came home that night he was in a very somber mood, having begun to see at last how those might be right who had laughed at him for his faith in America. . . .

On the Job

There was no heat upon the killing beds; the men might exactly as well have worked out of doors all winter. For that matter, there was very little heat anywhere in the building, except in the cooking rooms and such places—and it was the men who worked in these who ran the most risk of all, because whenever they had to pass to another room they had to go through ice-cold corridors, and sometimes with nothing on above the waist except a sleeveless undershirt. On the killing beds you were apt to be covered with blood, and it would freeze solid; if you leaned against a pillar, you would freeze to that, and if you put your hand upon the blade of your knife, you would run a chance of leaving your skin on it. The men would tie up their feet in newspapers and old sacks, and these would be soaked in blood and frozen, and then soaked again, and so on, until by nighttime a man would be walk-

ing on great lumps the size of the feet of an elephant. Now and
then, when the bosses were not looking, you would see them
plunging their feet and ankles into the steaming hot carcass of the
steer, or darting across the room to the hot-water jets. The cruelest
thing of all was that nearly all of them—all of those who used
knives—were unable to wear gloves, and their arms would be
white with frost and their hands would grow numb, and then of
course there would be accidents. Also the air would be full of
steam, from the hot water and the hot blood, so that you could not
see five feet before you; and then, with men rushing about at the
speed they kept up on the killing beds, and all with butcher knives,
like razors, in their hands—well, it was to be counted as a wonder that there were not more men slaughtered than cattle. . . .

One of the rules on the killing beds was that a man who was
one minute late was docked an hour, and this was economical,
for he was made to work the balance of the hour—he was not allowed to stand round and wait. And on the other hand if he came
ahead of time he got no pay for that—though often the bosses
would start up the gang ten or fifteen minutes before the whis-
tle. And this same custom they carried over to the end of the day;
they did not pay for any fraction of an hour—for "broken time."
A man might work full fifty minutes, but if there was no work to
fill out the hour, there was no pay for him. Thus the end of every
day was a sort of lottery—a struggle, all but breaking into open
war between the bosses and the men, the former trying to rush a
job through and the latter trying to stretch it out. . . .

The Inspectors

The people of Chicago saw the government inspectors in Packingtown, and they all took that to mean that they were protected
from diseased meat; they did not understand that these hundred
and sixty-three inspectors had been appointed at the request of
the packers, and that they were paid by the United States government to certify that all the diseased meat was kept in the state.
They had no authority beyond that; for the inspection of meat to
be sold in the city and state the whole force in Packingtown consisted of three henchmen of the local political machine! And
shortly afterward one of these, a physician, made the discovery
that the carcasses of steers which had been condemned as tubercular by the government inspectors, and which therefore contained ptomaines, which are deadly poisons, were left upon an

open platform and carted away to be sold in the city; and so he insisted that these carcasses be treated with an injection of kerosene—and was ordered to resign the same week! So indignant were the packers that they went farther, and compelled the mayor to abolish the whole bureau of inspection; so that since then there has not been even a pretence of any interference with the graft. There was said to be two thousand dollars a week hush money from the tubercular steers alone, and as much again from the hogs which had died of cholera on the trains, and which you might see any day being loaded into box cars and hauled away to a place called Globe, in Indiana, where they made a fancy grade of lard. . . .

There were cattle which had been fed on "whiskey malt," the refuse of the breweries, and had become what the men called "steerly"—which means covered with boils. It was a nasty job killing these, for when you plunged your knife into them they would burst and splash foul-smelling stuff into your face; and when a man's sleeves were smeared with blood, and his hands steeped in it, how was he ever to wipe his face, or to clear his eyes so that he could see? It was stuff such as this that made the "embalmed beef" that had killed several times as many United States soldiers as all the bullets of the Spaniards; only the army beef, besides, was not fresh canned, it was old stuff that had been lying for years in the cellars. . . .

The Horrors of Work

There were the men in the pickle rooms, for instance, where old Antanas had gotten his death; scarce a one of these that had not some spot of horror on his person. Let a man so much as scrape his finger pushing a truck in the pickle rooms, and he might have a sore that would put him out of the world; all the joints in his fingers might be eaten by the acid, one by one. Of the butchers and floorsmen, the beef boners and trimmers, and all those who used knives, you could scarcely find a person who had the use of his thumb; time and time again the base of it had been slashed, till it was a mere lump of flesh against which the man pressed the knife to hold it. The hands of these men would be crisscrossed with cuts, until you could no longer pretend to count them or to trace them. They would have no nails,—they had worn them off pulling hides; their knuckles were swollen so that their fingers spread out like a fan. There were men who worked in the cooking rooms, in the midst of steam and sickening odors, by artificial light; in these rooms the germs of tuberculosis might live for two years, but the supply was renewed every hour. There were the beef luggers, who carried two-hundred-pound quarters into the refrigerator cars, a fearful kind of work, that began at four o'clock in the morning, and that wore out the most powerful men in a few years. There were those who worked in the chilling rooms, and whose special disease was rheumatism; the time limit that a man could work in the chilling rooms was said to be five years. There were the wool pluckers, whose hands went to pieces even sooner than the hands of the pickle men; for the pelts of the sheep had to be painted with acid to loosen the wool, and then the pluckers had to pull out this wool with their bare hands, till the acid had eaten their fingers off. There were those who made the tins for the canned meat, and their hands, too, were a maze of cuts, and each cut represented a chance for blood poisoning. Some worked at the stamping machines, and it was very seldom that one could work long there at the pace that was set, and not give out and forget himself, and have a part of his hand chopped off. There were the "hoisters," as they were called, whose task it was to press the lever which lifted the dead cattle off the floor. They ran along upon a rafter, peering down through the damp and the steam, and as old Durham's architects had not built the killing room for the convenience of the hoisters, at every few feet they would have to stoop under a beam, say four feet above the one they ran on, which got them into the habit of stooping, so that in a few years they would be walking like chimpanzees. Worst of any, however, were the fertilizer men, and those who served in the cooking rooms. These people could not be shown to the visitor—for the odor of a fertilizer man would scare any ordinary visitor at a hundred yards, and as for the other men, who worked in tank rooms full of steam, and in some of which there were open vats near the level of the floor, their peculiar trouble was that they fell into the vats; and when they were fished out, there was never enough of them left to be worth exhibiting—sometimes they would be overlooked for days, till all but the bones of them had gone out to the world as Durham's Pure Leaf Lard!

The Long Shadow of Upton Sinclair

by Leon Harris

Leon Harris, a freelance writer and author of *The Fine Art of Political Wit*, discusses the importance of Upton Sinclair. Harris calls Sinclair "America's most important writer." He backs this up by contrasting American life before Sinclair with life after his writing, quoting a long list of people who were greatly influenced by Sinclair, and comparing the famous author with Ralph Nader, another crusader for consumer rights. He warns that because there are those in power who are corrupt, there will always be a need for crusaders like Sinclair.

Upton Sinclair was born on September 20, 1878, and died November 25, 1968. Until 1905, he was an unknown failure. For forty years thereafter he was America's most important writer; that is, he was more responsible than any other writer for the changing view Americans had of themselves, their rights, and their reasonable expectations. But by the time he died, Sinclair was again virtually unknown. . . .

I have not said that he was America's *best* writer, in the sense of having created the most enduring literature, although he was a better writer than he is presently taken to be, but the *most important*. By that I mean that the effects of his writing have been and still are more important than those of any other American professional writer.

Perhaps one at least partial definition of great art may be that art which lasts—which continues to be moving to succeeding

Leon Harris, *Upton Sinclair: American Rebel*. New York: Thomas Y. Crowell Company, 1975.
Copyright © 1975 by Leon Harris. Reproduced by permission.

generations. Art that is not great, even if it is thought so initially, eventually disappears from public view and interest.

Great propaganda, on the other hand, must be just the opposite; it must so convince the public that its ideas or attitudes become generally accepted; so commonplace, in fact, that they are taken for granted and the propaganda itself disappears from memory. When people attribute to their own good sense or to the natural order of things an idea that was first or best proposed by a propagandist—and have forgotten him—it was successful propaganda.

Sinclair originated *none* of the ideas for which he propagandized, nor did he claim to have. But he convinced millions of people all over the world of them. Other of his contemporary muckrakers played a greater role than he in effecting particular social change. But not one of them approached his total influence in regard to all the ideas he advocated. In the variety of his work and in his incomparable success in having it widely reprinted, discussed, attacked, and kept in print, Sinclair outweighed all other individual muckrakers.

When President Theodore Roosevelt in 1906 first called these reformers "muckrakers," he meant it to be derogatory, but they seized the name and used it themselves proudly. With the passing years it has, however, come to be vaguely synonymous with yellow journalists.

Nor did Sinclair only sit and write. He took courageous physical and political action to advance his causes, was used by Presidents and used them in turn. His own life was as exciting as that of most of his heroes.

When Sinclair became an important writer at the beginning of the century, there was no minimum wage, no maximum working hours, no employer liability for accidents, no pure food and drug laws, no right to bargain collectively, no strong unions, no votes and, as a practical matter, no rights for women, no education permitted on birth control or venereal disease, no effective anti-price-fixing activity, no health insurance or social security or unemployment compensation, and no supervision of banks or stock exchanges or insurance companies. These are only a few of the areas in which Sinclair's propaganda helped to bring about reform.

More important even than the lack of legislation were the attitudes of most Americans—might makes right, *caveat emptor*, the end justifies the means—simple social Darwinism and devil take the hindmost. By the end of Sinclair's ninety years, the attitudes of the majority of Americans had so changed that curative legislation had been enacted, was generally supposed to be enforced, and was, as a matter of fact, too much taken for granted.

Sinclair's was a time when writers were important, when America had no television. A single book or article of his could reach millions more people than would see and hear the most hard-working politician-lecturer, such as Eugene V. Debs, in his whole lifetime.

Because of the ephemeral nature of great propaganda, it is very difficult to assess a propagandist's direct influence on specific individuals through his own works; but it is even harder to identify his influence extended by others affected by him. Nevertheless, I have tried to trace his effect through other men and women who themselves have had an important influence of their own on this country and elsewhere. Because Sinclair believed that reform was possible in virtually every institution of America, he wrote about them all, and I have quoted throughout this book from specialists in each field regarding his influence on them. But in this Introduction, I quote a few merely to indicate the almost unbelievable breadth of that influence.

Eric Sevareid [newsman]: "He was one of those figures from the great muckraking days . . . who excited me as a young student . . . to become a journalist."

Dr. Karl Menninger [psychiatrist]: "Sinclair's *Jungle*, read to me as a teenager, produced a profound effect, a kind of horror regarding the inhumanity of man to man."

Robert McNamara [former secretary of defense]: "He did influence me in my thinking by identifying three or four decades ago many of the problems which because they remain unresolved are dividing our nation today."

Allen Ginsberg [poet]: "Sinclair influenced my family, i.e., 20's and thirties radicalism was sustained by his common sense & good heart. . . . Hindsight in the 60's made his economic & political activities seem charming prefigurations of present youth rebellion."

Daniel Patrick Moynihan [politician]: "Sinclair was much in my mind when I began to work on traffic safety problems in the late 1950's. . . . This development—I brought Ralph Nader to Washington to work on the subject when I became Assistant Secretary of Labor under Kennedy—did, I think, lead to important legislation."

Norman Mailer [novelist]: "Upton Sinclair had no particular influence on my life except in one way and that was not small. I read his novel, BOSTON, when I was 12 or 13 and hardly understood it, but for better or worse it moved me to the left. I still remember the portrait of Vanzetti."

Writers as unlikely as Moss Hart and George S. Kaufman, journalists with audiences as great as Walter Cronkite and William Shirer, politicians and political activists, blacks as well as whites, all attest to Sinclair's direct effect on their lives.

The indirect effects (those ever-expanding circles) of a propagandist on individuals are even harder to measure, but sometimes not impossible.

John Kenneth Galbraith [economist]: "I expect like others I was influenced by him but I am sure at second or third hand."

Ramsey Clark [former attorney general of the United States]: "I have sensed a powerful influence of Upton Sinclair on many people whom I respect. . . . His influence on those who most strongly influenced us was undoubtedly great."

Outside of America, Sinclair's effect on those who influenced others is also traceable. Bertolt Brecht was clearly influenced by Sinclair and, in fact, was in touch with him through Elizabeth Hauptmann. The millions of copies of Sinclair's books published in the Soviet Union registered on its artists great and small from Sergei Eisenstein to Aleksandr Solzhenitsyn. . . . One may hope that the Republic will continue to produce writers like Sinclair, who will help keep its citizens from becoming short of breath or losing their good humor in the endless opposition to injustice. Such writers provide one of the answers to the question, "What can one person do?"

Sinclair and Nader

Shortly before his eighty-eighth birthday, Sinclair and May [his wife Mary] lunched at the White House with Mrs. Lyndon Johnson. At eighty-nine, he returned to the White House to watch President Johnson sign the Wholesome Meat Act of 1967, designed to plug some of the loopholes in the 1906 law for whose passage *The Jungle* had been chiefly responsible.

Lyndon Johnson was scarcely less obsessed with getting good personal publicity than Sinclair himself. He had, therefore, also brought to that White House signing consumer advocate Ralph Nader, who like Upton and perhaps like most men did not overestimate the achievements of others as compared to his own. "I sort of felt," Nader said later of the encounter with Sinclair, "that two historic consumer ages were meeting. . . . Maybe this time, I thought, the work will have some effect."

Despite Nader's probably unconscious minimizing, the work of the earlier time, of course, had not only "some effect" but an enormous one. In fact, it is impossible to imagine Ralph Nader as anything more than just another unknown and unsuccessful crank had not Sinclair and the many other muckrakers been fighting the fight for the previous sixty years. It was they who had created, organized, and led the public demand that had brought about both the laws and the agencies to enforce those laws to protect citizens. The point of view of most Americans in the days of Jurgis Rudkus had been one of more or less patient acceptance. It was the muckrakers, and chief among them Sinclair, who had transformed the climate in America into an ever-increasing demand by the public for social justice and consumer protection as a matter of right.

Evidences of this changed climate abound, most significantly perhaps, in the fact that an increasing number of American corporations present some sort of social accounting not only in their advertising to the public but also in their annual reports to stockholders. . . .

The Muckrakers Then and Now

Similarly, the regular reporting in newspapers and on television of business abuses is also a tribute to the muckrakers' effectiveness, because before their efforts, such matters were scrupulously avoided in the press.

Corporations are not in serious danger of overemphasizing social responsibilities at the expense of profits and there is a continuing pattern of business atrocities. In the field of Sinclair's most famous fight, spoiled, adulterated, and misrepresented foods, there are also still almost daily proofs that the fight, far from being over, is as endless as human greed. But that variants of these abuses continue is not surprising. What is perhaps surprising and gratifying is the recent increased interest both in what has come to be called consumerism and in a balanced ecology. Of course, some businessmen still collude to fix prices and avoid competition and some still bribe politicians. Some citizens are still too rich and overpaid and others too poor and underpaid. Nor is it any longer only those who have always had the greatest power or money who are cheating, but also many laborers now cheat the public with shoddy work, protected by the powerful unions and unemployment benefits Sinclair fought for. Indeed, big and corrupt unions have now joined big and corrupt businesses as appropriate and everyday targets for the latest generation of muckrakers.

The triumph of that technology which Sinclair believed should improve the human condition has intensified and complicated the problem of who will control that technology and how—a problem he insisted could be handled by "industrial democracy," which has yet to be tried.

All this merely proves that a generally higher standard of living does not by and of itself produce Eden, but thanks to Sinclair and others, many of whom were inspired by him, the rules of the game are somewhat stricter.

Uncle Tom's Cabin, The Jungle, and *Grapes of Wrath* are the three most effective muckraking novels in America's history to date. But the future should see comparable works, indeed America seems likely, unless dictatorship prevents it, to witness even more muckraking than in the past. There are now more media, there is a wider audience, and there are also more subjects, for nothing is sacred any more and therefore nothing is above criticism. That the muckrakers of today and of the future owe a debt to Sinclair and to others influenced by him is indisputable. As the Washington *Post* reported: "What Drew Pearson writes in the newspapers and Ralph Nader writes in the magazines, what James Ridgeway writes in *The New Republic* and I.F. Stone in his newsletter is directly traceable to the muckraking tradition of American journalism. It is a tradition built upon outrage, and an almost Talmudic interpretation of ethics. The classic practitioners of the art were Lincoln Steffens, Jacob Riis and Upton Sinclair . . . the most famous of the three. . . . When today the public is informed about the financial machinations of Senator Dodd by Pearson, or American automobiles by Nader, or the universities by Ridgeway, or the military-industrial complex by Stone, it ought to understand that it owes a debt to the Sinclairs, the Steffenses, and the Riises. They were the men who pioneered the art form, who saw injustice and tried to right it, who believed absolutely in the wonderful cleansing properties of the embarrassing fact, bluntly disclosed."

Praise for Sinclair

Sinclair had lived so long and done so much that in the 1950's and 1960's it was as though he were seeing the movie again. Books of his published as early as 1904 and 1906 were being reprinted and reviewed by a whole new generation. Some of these new critics pointed out that the New Deal and subsequent prosperity had stolen his thunder, to which he replied mildly: "Someone has remarked that 'the business of people with ideas is to have them stolen,' and I was happy to be robbed by two presidents, Theodore and Franklin D. Roosevelt."

Although some found Sinclair's ideas old-hat, others judged them to be unfortunately more relevant than ever and now not only on an American but a worldwide scale. The critic Harvey Swados wrote: "*The Jungle* must renew its hold on the imaginations of an entirely new generation of readers.

". . . We are entering a new time. We sense uneasily that we do not have it made, that with . . . prosperity have come new and staggering problems, and that there is a vast suffering world beyond our national boundaries, struggling in a variety of ways to accumulate capital and thus to move, as we have moved, up into the twentieth century. We sense, too, that throughout this world, no matter how the capital is accumulated . . . it is being done at a stupendous cost in human suffering. There is a close parallel between the payment in hunger, blood, and agony of the peoples of the underdeveloped world and that extracted from the immigrant builders of the American empire.

"It is a parallel that we will neglect only at our own peril; it is one that should fill us with humility and compassion for all who must strain like beasts of the field to bring the world to the next epoch; it is one that *The Jungle* will help to sustain in the forefront of our consciousness, which is where it belongs. To the extent that it fulfills this function, this book now begins a new and vital existence as a force in the spiritual and social lives of a new and, it is to be hoped, a responsible generation of readers."

For a man who had been in turn ignored, ridiculed, and maligned, it was sweet now on occasion to see himself apotheosized. "Upton Sinclair is of the American type most brilliantly exemplified by Jefferson, the two Roosevelts and possibly, Kennedy— he was a traitor to his class," declared Gerald W. Johnson, "a propagandist miles above Thomas Paine and Henry George, and not far below Aquinas, Erasmus and Voltaire. Propagandists are kittle cattle; critics and historians have never known how to classify them. Zola couldn't write, but he wrecked a social order. Socrates never wrote at all, but he wrecked a world. Upton Sinclair . . . has shaped the thinking of millions who never heard of any other American writer."

Picasso Paints *Les Demoiselles d'Avignon:*
1907

Picasso Creates a New Art Form

by Arianna Stassinopoulos Huffington

Arianna Stassinopoulos Huffington is a writer, lecturer, and broadcaster who has written several books including *The Female Woman, After Reason, Maria Callas,* and *The Gods of Greece.* Huffington writes of the remarkable year 1907 when Picasso painted *Les Demoiselles d'Avignon,* which brought about a revolutionary new art form—cubism. She believes Picasso is important for his new approaches to art as well as the way he mirrors the past century's beliefs and attitudes. She tells how Picasso and others created cubism as a revolution against art of the past.

S omething else had been awakened in him in Gosol and was fed, back in Paris, by the growing enthusiasm around him for primitive art. The primitive-art departments at the Louvre and in the Trocadéro's museum of ethnography were receiving more and more attention, and many of his artist friends started buying masks and primitive statuettes from bric-a-brac dealers. Especially Matisse and [French painter and sculptor] André Derain, who, a little over a year older than Picasso, had recently moved to Montmartre and joined the *bande* at the Bateau-Lavoir. His favorite occupation, when he was not painting, was talking about painting. [French poet André] Salmon, in fact, accused him of "trying to force his friends to speculate on the whole problem of art every time they took a brush in their hands." In 1906, it was the problem of African and Oriental art on which he wanted his friends to speculate.

Arianna Stassinopoulos Huffington, *Picasso: Creator and Destroyer.* New York: Simon and Schuster, 1988. Copyright © 1988 by Arianna Stassinopoulos Huffington. Reproduced by permission of Arthur Pine Associates, Inc., New York, NY.

"On the Rue de Rennes," wrote Matisse, "I often passed the shop of Père Sauvage. There were Negro statuettes in his window. I was struck by their character, their purity of line. It was as fine as Egyptian art. So I bought one and showed it to Gertrude Stein, whom I was visiting that day. And then Picasso arrived. He took to it immediately." [French writer and painter] Max Jacob's recollection was much more dramatic. "Matisse took a black wooden statuette off a table and showed it to Picasso. Picasso held it in his hands all evening. The next morning, when I came to his studio, the floor was strewn with sheets of drawing paper. Each sheet had virtually the same drawing on it, a big woman's face with a single eye, a nose too long that merged into the mouth, a lock of hair on the shoulder. Cubism was born."

Cubism was not yet born, but in the fall and winter of 1906, Picasso was definitely pregnant with it. And preparations were under way for the momentous event. He had a canvas mounted on specially strong material as reinforcement and ordered a stretcher of massive dimensions. Years later he talked to [French writer and political activist] André Malraux of the moment of conception: "All alone in that awful museum, with masks, dolls made by the redskins, dusty manikins. *Les Demoiselles d'Avignon* must have come to me that very day, but not at all because of the forms; because it was my first exorcism-painting—yes absolutely . . . When I went to the old Trocadéro, it was disgusting. The Flea Market. The smell. I was all alone. I wanted to get away. But I didn't leave. I stayed. I stayed. I understood that it was very important: something was happening to me, right? The masks weren't just like any other pieces of sculpture. Not at all. They were magic things. But why weren't the Egyptian pieces or the Chaldean? We hadn't realized it. Those were primitives, not magic things. The Negro pieces were *intercesseurs*, mediators; ever since then I've known the word in French. They were against everything—against unknown, threatening spirits. I always looked at fetishes. I understood; I too am against everything. I too believe that everything is unknown, that everything is an enemy! Everything! Not the details—women, children, babies, tobacco, playing—but the whole of it! I understood what the Negroes used their sculpture for. Why sculpt like that and not some other way? After all, they weren't Cubists! Since Cubism didn't exist. It was clear that some guys had invented the models, and others had imitated them, right? Isn't that what we call tradition? But all the fetishes were used for the same thing. They were weapons. To help people avoid coming under the influence of spirits again, to help them become independent. They're tools. If we give spirits a form, we become independent. Spirits, the unconscious (people still weren't talking about that very much), emotion—they're all the same thing. I understood why I was a painter."

Art as Destruction

Everything, the whole of creation, was an enemy, and he was a painter in order to fashion not works of art—he always despised the use of that term—but weapons: defensive weapons against surrendering to the spell of the spirit that fills creation, and weapons of combat against everything outside man, against every emotion of belonging in creation, against nature, human nature, and the God who created it all. "Obviously," he said, "nature has to exist so that we may rape it!"

It was a thoroughly destructive art manifesto, but it was accepted, integrated and bought, partly because it mirrored the destruction of the most destructive of all centuries, and partly because it was interpreted as a lesser destructiveness and a smaller rejection, not of "the whole of it" but, depending on the interpreter, of bourgeois society, traditional art, sexual inhibitions, outdated mores and conventions. So his ultimate message was ignored or laundered until it was seen only as an audacious call to liberate art and society from all shackles.

It was more, much more, than that. It was a rejection of life and creation, which he saw as inescapably dark and harrowingly evil, an evil that was the product not merely of man and political systems but of the forces behind creation. So there was no hope beyond this existential rejection,—no light beyond the anonymous, merciless darkness, no beauty beyond the ugliness and no new morning of creation beyond the suspended apocalypse. It was all—"the whole of it"—closed, condemned and damned.

There was, fortunately, another world of beauty, tenderness and an almost pastoral vision to which he could sometimes retreat, both in his work and in his life. There was no border between the two worlds and no redemption to be found, but at least the existence of that other world enabled him to survive the orgy of destructiveness that he was about to unleash in his work.

Les Demoiselles d'Avignon may have come to Picasso in the

Trocadéro, but there were Iberian influences, Egyptian influences and many unconscious philosophical influences whose principal perpetrator was a man scarcely five feet tall with long black hair parted on his large head and falling on his narrow shoulders, and with mad, deep black eyes. It was Alfred Jarry, the creator of Father Ubu, who in his play *Ubu Roi* summed up his philosophy of destruction: "Hornsocket! We will not have demolished everything if we don't demolish even the ruins!" Jarry abhorred every aspect of contemporary society, its bourgeois pretensions, sham and hypocrisy, and his life no less than his art was devoted to its destruction. He carried a pair of pistols and contrived opportunities to use them to underscore his social role. When someone stopped him in the street one night and asked him for a light, Jarry murmured politely, "Voilà," while pulling his gun and producing a flash of light by shooting it in the air.

He had given Picasso a Browning automatic, which he loved to carry and use on similarly inappropriate occasions. He fired it in the air with particular relish once as an answer to some admirers' persistent questioning about his "theory of aesthetics." The admirers were silenced, and Picasso wallowed in his display of outrageousness, which, as Jarry had been preaching, whether practiced in art or in life, helped push the frontiers of art and society beyond the present contemptible reality.

Destructiveness was Jarry's rallying call, and a deep, barbaric destructiveness was at the center of *Les Demoiselles d'Avignon*. But even as Picasso was working on the *Demoiselles*, Jarry, only thirty-four years old, lay on his deathbed, having destroyed himself with alcohol and ether before he had succeeded in destroying society. The man whom Apollinaire had described as "the last of the sublime debauchees in an orgy of intelligence" surrendered to a longing deeper than his flamboyant mind just before he died and asked for a priest to administer the last rites. The arch-cynic who had declared that "God is the shortest path from zero to infinity . . . therefore, ultimately, the point tangential to both," felt compelled on his deathbed to seek that God's presence in the most time-honored and conventional form. It was only one more paradox in a life filled with paradox. The man who had lived and died a virgin had, in his plays, often set the raw sexuality and primitive power of black Africans against the decadence and bankruptcy of their rulers. And in *Les Demoiselles d'Avi-*

gnon, Picasso, no less obsessed with raw sexuality for liberally indulging in it, chose, as André Salmon put it, savage artists as guides. He was "the apprentice sorcerer always consulting the Oceanic and African enchanters."

When Jarry gave Picasso his own revolver, he knew that he had found the man who would carry out his mission of destruction. It was a ritual act and was seen as such by all those present at the supper at which Jarry passed on the sacred symbol. "The revolver," wrote Max Jacob, "sought its natural owner . . . It was really the harbinger comet of the new century." So was the explosion that was named *Les Demoiselles d'Avignon*: five horrifying women, prostitutes who repel rather than attract and whose faces are primitive masks that challenge not only society but humanity itself. Even the Picasso *bande* was horrified. "It was the ugliness of the faces," wrote Salmon, "that froze with horror the half-converted." Apollinaire murmured revolution; [with his sister Gertrude, a collector and patron of modern painters] Leo Stein burst into embarrassed, uncomprehending laughter; Gertrude Stein lapsed into unaccustomed silence; Matisse swore revenge on this barbaric mockery of modern painting and Derain expressed his wry concern that "one day Picasso would be found hanging behind his big picture."

"It is not necessary," Picasso later said, "to paint a man with a gun. An apple can be just as revolutionary." And so can a brothel. [French painter] Georges Braque, who had just met Picasso when he saw *Les Demoiselles d'Avignon* in the fall of 1907, knew immediately that nothing less than a revolution was intended. "It made me feel," he said, "as if someone was drinking gasoline and spitting fire." He was shocked, but he was also stirred as he had never been before. . . .

From the time that he shook the art world with *Les Demoiselles d'Avignon*, Picasso was out of love with the world. He saw his role as a painter as fashioning weapons of combat against every emotion of belonging in creation and celebrating life, against nature, human nature and the God who created it all. "I must obstinately remain at the moment among those who cannot see Picasso in the ultimate pantheon," wrote the artist and art critic Michael Ayrton in 1956. "If he is not here it is because whilst the whole achievement is miraculous I am conscious of a factor missing which is present in ultimately great painting, and this factor is the depth which accompanies ineloquence. The still centre."

"How difficult it is," Picasso had said soon after his eighty-fifth birthday, "to get something of the absolute into the frog pond." But however difficult, is it not the highest function of art to try to get something of the absolute into the frog pond of this world? With prodigious skill, complete mastery of the language of painting, inexhaustible versatility and monumental virtuosity, ingenuity and imagination, Picasso showed us the mud in our frog pond and the night over it. There is, of course, "no sun without shadow, and it is essential to know the night," yet there is a sense in all great art that beyond the darkness and the nightmares that it portrays, beyond humanity's anguished cries that it gives voice to, there is harmony, order and peace. There is fear in Shakespeare's *Tempest* and in Mozart's *Magic Flute*, but it is cast out by love; there is horror and ugliness, but a new order of harmony and beauty evolves out of them; there is evil, but it is overcome by good. "Despite so many ordeals," cries out Oedipus, "my advanced age and the nobility of my soul make me conclude that all is well."

Picasso's advanced age was filled with despair and fueled by hatred. As for his art, he had told André Malraux that "he had no need of style, because his rage would become a prime factor in the style of our time." And his rage did become the dominant style of our time; but there are growing signs that something beyond rage is demanded by the present. "Modern artists," [art historian] Meyer Schapiro wrote, "have greater resources than modernity allows them to disclose—resources which are often unsuspected by the artists themselves." It was a call to modern artists to explore the worlds that would be revealed "if their art were open to all that they felt or loved."

Cubism Becomes a Radical Departure for Twentieth-Century Art

by John Richardson with Marilyn McCully

John Richardson is an art critic who knew Picasso. He has organized various art exhibitions and has written on artists such as Edouard Manet and Georges Braque. Marilyn McCully is a noted Picasso scholar who has published many books and articles on the artist. She has also organized exhibits of his works. In the following selection Richardson and McCully explore cubism—what it stood against and what it stood for, according to Picasso and Braque. According to the authors, Picasso's cubism totally changed the way an artist could represent reality and brought out of it every important modernist movement.

T he word "cubism" started life as a meaningless epithet, which had as little relevance to the art it has come to denote as the caricatures of the works that appeared in humor magazines. However, it caught on with the public; even with Braque and Picasso, who loathed the word for the reason that it did not

John Richardson with Marilyn McCully, *A Life of Picasso, Volume II: 1907–1917*. New York: Random House, 1996. Copyright © 1991 by John Richardson Fine Arts Ltd. Reproduced by permission of the publisher.

apply to what they were doing but soon found themselves obliged to use it. Over the years "cubism" has achieved universal acceptance by virtue of designating

> the most important and certainly the most complete and radical artistic revolution since the Renaissance. . . . [Nothing] has so altered the principles, so shaken the foundations of Western painting as did Cubism. Indeed, from a visual point of view it is easier to bridge the three hundred and fifty years separating Impressionism from the High Renaissance than it is to bridge the fifty years that lie between Impressionism and Cubism. . . . A portrait by Renoir will seem closer to a portrait by Raphael than it does to a Cubist portrait by Picasso. . . .

Before seeing what cubism stands for, let us see what it stood against. For Picasso cubism constituted, among other things, a reaction against impressionism, whose two great luminaries, Renoir and Monet, were still hard at work and by now venerated by the public which had once ridiculed them. Picasso's attitude to impressionism was irreverent and ironical, not to say iconoclastic. . . .

However, it was not so much these elderly impressionists that Picasso and Braque were in revolt against as the whole outmoded concept of impressionism; the lack of substance inherent in the very term; the flimsy art-for-art's-sake shimmer of impressionist light effects. Cubism was also a reaction against the followers of the impressionists: against the methodology of the divisionists, the garishness of fauvism, and, in Picasso's case, against his pet aversion, Bonnard. "A potpourri of indecision" is how he described this artist's work. He had caught his fear of melting in the bath like a piece of soap from Bonnard, he said. . . .

Value of Cubism

As the critic Roger Allard saw, as early as 1912, cubism was a means of registering "mass, volume and weight." Henceforth, everything had to be tactile and palpable, not least space. Palpability made for reality, and it was the real rather than the realistic that Picasso was out to capture. A cup or a jug or a pair of binoculars should not be a copy of the real thing, it need not even look like the real thing; it simply had to be as real as the real thing. And so there would be no more falsehoods; no more three-dimensional simulation, no more artful trompe l'œil effects, except for the famous trompe l'œil nail with a shadow that Braque added to more than one of his 1909 still lifes in order to contrast the eye-fooling mendacity of traditional notation with the cubists' realistic treatment of forms in space.

"When we invented cubism," Picasso remarked many years later, "we had no intention whatever of inventing cubism. We simply wanted to express what was in us." Braque said more or less the same thing. "Cubism, or rather my cubism, was a means that I created for my own use, whose primary aim was to put painting within the range of my own gifts." Both artists were loath to define what their cubism was really about. Nevertheless, at one time or another, both came out with explanations. As one might expect, Picasso's pronouncements tend to be paradoxical and contradictory: "there is no such thing as cubism," he told one interviewer and excused himself to feed his monkey. Braque, however, was more forthcoming and articulate, and it is to him we have to turn for enlightenment as to the techniques that they employed at this first so-called analytic phase of cubism. This is how Braque explains his abandonment of perspective:

> Traditional perspective gave me no satisfaction. It is too mechanical to allow one to take full possession of things. It has its origins in a single viewpoint and never gets away from it. But the viewpoint is of little importance. It is as if someone spent his life drawing profiles and believed that man was one-eyed. When we arrived at this conclusion, everything changed, you have no idea how much.

It followed that if the artist was ever "to take full possession of things," he must be able to represent an object from any number of viewpoints at the same time. Multiple views in one form or another recur throughout cubism; however, they are only one of Braque and Picasso's radical innovations. No less revolutionary was their reduction of the spatial element to an ever shallower recession; this enabled them to bring everything as near as possible to the surface of the canvas and as near as possible to us. Braque described this manner of dealing with space as "tactile" or "manual," because it enabled him "to make people want to touch what has been painted as well as look at it." It is a complete reversal of the time-honored system of establishing a distance and making objects recede from us. To bring things within our grasp, Braque (and Picasso) took to fragmenting and faceting forms, because "this was a means of getting as close to the objects as painting allowed. Fragmentation allowed me to establish a spatial element as well as a spatial movement and until this had been achieved I was not able to introduce objects into my pictures." In the same way, faceting allowed the artist (much as it does a man who cuts gemstones) to use refracted light to give his surfaces a generalized sparkle. This was a tremendous advance on the traditional device of a single source of light.

Braque's L'Estaque landscapes set in motion a process that would totally change the way an artist represents things: a process that would enable Braque and Picasso to come up with an art that would be "simultaneously representational and antinaturalistic," and thus make modernism possible. Over the years this art would come to be divided into two phases: analytic and (after the invention of papier collé) synthetic cubism. Given their deep distrust of art historians, Picasso and Braque never took their categories very seriously. However, cubism does lend itself to this convenient, albeit arbitrary, categorization, so we are obliged to use it. Analytic cubism permitted the two artists to take things apart: dissect them "with the practiced and methodical hand of a great surgeon" (as Apollinaire said of Picasso). It enabled their followers to make a further breakthrough: into the realm of abstraction—a breakthrough that they themselves would always hold back from making. Analytic cubism would make possible the achievements of de Stijl, constructivism and even minimalism. Synthetic cubism, on the other hand, permitted Picasso and Braque to put things together again, to create images and objects in a revolutionary new way, out of whatever materials they chose. It would thus make possible the achievements of the dadaists, the surrealists, even the pop artists. No question about it, cubism engendered every major modernist movement.

Rutherford's Experiments Revolutionize Atomic Research

by Sarah R. Riedman

Sarah R. Riedman, Ph.D. from Columbia University, was an author, lecturer, and an assistant professor of biology at Brooklyn College. She tells the story of Ernest Rutherford, a research student who started out under the tutelage of J.J. Thompson, the discoverer of the electron. Rutherford and Thompson investigated X rays and other forms of radiation. Rutherford was appointed chief researcher at McGill University in Montreal, Canada, where he continued his research into radioactivity. Later he accepted an offer to conduct research at the University of Manchester in England, where he ran a lab with fifteen research workers. In 1908 he was awarded the Nobel Prize in chemistry for investigating the decay of radioactive elements. In the following excerpt Riedman explains what Rutherford did in 1911 that revolutionized physics. He investigated the structure of atoms by bombarding gold foil with alpha particles. He found that the particles were occasionally bouncing back as if having collided with something solid. He calculated that the atom was composed of a nucleus surrounded by a sphere of electrification. This discovery changed forever how people understood the primary elements of the universe.

Sarah R. Riedman, *Men and Women Behind the Atom*. London: Abelard-Schuman Limited, 1958. Copyright © 1958 by Sarah R. Riedman. Reproduced by permission.

Everywhere, he [Rutherford] was the great figure who dominated atomic science of his day. There were other awards, honors, and medals including one from the National Academy of Sciences in the United States. Dr. Nicholas Murray Butler, then president of Columbia University, brought the medal to England, and presented it in person.

Rutherford didn't rest on his laurels. Another epoch-making event, his crowning achievement, was in the making. From a number of his letters and papers it is known that the structure of the atom was very much in his thinking. To Professor W.H. Bragg, who had gone from Cambridge to Adelaide, Australia, and who was now at Leeds in England, he wrote in 1911:

> Did I tell you that Hahn finds that the penetrating beta rays from a simple product are not homogeneous . . . ? I think I can offer an explanation of that. . . . I can see that the working out of a complete theory of the alpha and beta rays is going to be rather a large job; but the outlook is very promising. . . .

What was the inside of the atom like? Rutherford was not the first of brilliant physicists to ask the question. In fact, there were several answers which took the form of 'models.' The physicist's model is nothing you can touch, see or feel. It is a picture of an idea, but the idea must be tested by experiment. The German physicist, Philipp Lenard, at the University of Heidelberg, thought the atom was made up of 'dynamids'—a name he gave to an electron and a positive charge, pairs of which were supposed to be scattered through a large space in the atom. How did he arrive at this idea? He found that while a very small part of the atom stopped swift cathode rays, the major part of it permitted them to get through as if through empty space.

On the other hand, J.J. Thompson conceived the atom to be a sphere of positive electrification, in which the electrons, arranged in rings, were imbedded. On the matter of the atom's structure, teacher and pupil disagreed. The pupil expressed his idea in a famous paper, 'The Scattering of Alpha and Beta Particles of Matter and the Structure of the Atom.' In it, Rutherford described the results of a series of experiments on the bombardment of gold foil with beams of alpha particles. When a stream of alpha particles was fired at a thin sheet of foil, most of the particles passed through. So far, the observation was the same as others had noted. What was different?

Some of the particles, he found, were turned aside slightly, emerging from the gold foil at a small angle from their original path. But a few were deflected by large angles; what's more, an occasional particle actually came back, emerging from the same side of the foil it went in!

The genius of Rutherford is shown by the fact that this phenomenon gave him pause. Where others might have regarded these occasional bounce backs as minor accidents of the experiment, Rutherford wrote: 'It was quite the most incredible event that ever happened to me in my life. It was almost as incredible as if you had fired a 15-inch shell at a piece of tissue paper and it came back and hit you.' These deflections which he observed were much larger than could possibly be accounted for by either the Lenard or Thompson model. And so Rutherford proposed his own.

He pictured the atom as composed of a central charge (only later was this to be called the nucleus) surrounded by a sphere of electrification of equal but opposite charge. At this time, too, he wasn't sure whether the charge was positive or negative. 'For convenience,' he said, 'the sign will be assumed positive.' From his measurements of the particles that bounced back from the foil, or were deflected through a large angle, he calculated the probable size of the central core, and the diameter of the surrounding space. He found that the number of particles turned back by the foil was proportional to the atomic weight of the material and the thickness of the foil. He assumed that the size of the atom's central charge was proportional to its atomic weight. And so his model was indeed a simple one: a central core of electric charge, which we now call the nucleus, surrounded by a sphere of electrification which he later discovered was negative.

The nucleus of hydrogen has a charge of 1, the nucleus of helium 2, of lithium 3, and of plutonium 94. We call these the *atomic numbers*—the number of unit positive charges on the atomic nuclei of an element. A student of Heidelberg (at that time) writing today says: 'The paper produced no kind of sensation in the world of physics.' Apparently, Rutherford himself, though sure of his results, did not realize at the time, 'the supreme importance they were to have.' Two years later, writing about the structure of the nucleus, he said: 'No doubt the positively charged center of the atom is a complicated system in movement, consisting in part of charged helium and hydrogen atoms,' and further: 'It would appear as if the positively charged atoms of matter attract one another at very small distances, for otherwise it is difficult to see how the component parts at the center are held together.' Forty years later, it is still not clear what force holds these charges together.

While the world did not at first recognize the full significance of Rutherford's greatest discovery, one man who came to Manchester from Copenhagen, Denmark immediately saw the prospects of further discovery which were opened up as a result of the new atomic model. This man was Niels Bohr. There were some 'kinks' which needed 'ironing out.' While working in Rutherford's laboratory for several months he published a paper in 1912, in which he established the structure of the atom—a nucleus surrounded by electrons.

**Ernest Rutherford Discovers the Structure
of the Atomic Nucleus: 1911**

Rutherford's Legacy

by E.N. da C. Andrade

E.N. da C. Andrade was the author of many widely used books
dealing with physics and physicists. He was a professor of physics
at the University of London. In the following excerpt, Andrade tells
of the importance of Ernest Rutherford, who came up with the theory that all atoms had small electrically charged cores and a field of
surrounding electrical particles. This discovery led to the understanding that the atom was capable of tremendous changes; before
his death Rutherford predicted the possibility of obtaining huge
amounts of energy from nuclear reactions. Andrade also points out
that Rutherford was a mentor for other prominent physicists, including Otto Hahn, who a few years later showed how the uranium nucleus could be split.

We live in an atomic age, when the possibility of procur-
ing energy from the transmutation of atoms holds out,
on the one hand, a promise of easy prosperity and, on
the other hand, of universal destruction. The structure of the
atom, which little more than fifty years ago was, like the existence of life on the planets, a matter of occasional conjecture, is
now the subject of study of thousands, or tens of thousands, of
accomplished and highly trained men of science and a source of
expense exceeding that of the maintenance of the world's armies
and navies in the old days. All this derives directly from the work
of Ernest Rutherford.

The great astronomer Arthur S. Eddington said that in 1911

E.N. da C. Andrade, *Rutherford and the Nature of the Atom*. New York: Doubleday & Company, 1964. Copyright © 1964 by Educational Services Incorporated. Reproduced by permission of the author.

Rutherford introduced the greatest change in our ideas of matter since the time of Democritus—and Democritus lived four hundred years before Christ. He was referring to Rutherford's theory, put forward in that year, that every atom consisted of a very small electrically charged core, in which practically all its mass was concentrated, surrounded by a structure of electrical particles. The core was called the nucleus. At the time the notion of an atomic nucleus seemed fantastic to many; today the structure of this incredibly minute nucleus is intensely studied in leading laboratories all over the world. . . . Mainly under his inspiration, the study of atomic structure, of atomic transmutation, and of atomic energy developed to a point where the extraordinary advances of recent years were foreshadowed. . . .

It is certain that Rutherford is one of the greatest figures in the history of science. He is responsible for the modern belief that the atom, far from being a stable structure, is capable of changes of fundamental significance, in some cases spontaneous, in other cases provoked by means that he was the first to devise. . . .

Rutherford was a man of extraordinary scientific foresight, as instanced particularly in his anticipation of the neutron and of the isotopes of hydrogen and helium. It is sometimes asked if Rutherford foresaw, as a result of his work, the atomic bomb and the wholesale release of nuclear energy in general. In a lecture given in 1936, the year before he died, he referred to the possibility of obtaining energy on an industrial scale (he did not speak, or apparently think, of a bomb) from nuclear transmutation, saying, "While the over-all efficiency of the process rises with increase of energy of the bombarding particle, there seems to be little hope of gaining useful energy from the atoms by such methods. On the other hand, the recent discovery of the neutron and the proof of its extraordinary effectiveness in producing transmutations at very low velocities opens up new possibilities, if only a method could be found of producing slow neutrons in quantity with little expenditure of energy. At the moment, however, the natural radioactive bodies are the only known source for generating energy from atomic nuclei, but this is on far too small a scale to be useful for technical purposes." In his little book *The Newer Alchemy*, published in the following year, he said much the same, adding, "The outlook for gaining useful energy from the atoms by artificial processes of transformation does not look very promising." He did not, then, contemplate the possibility of any planned large-scale release of atomic energy in the near future, although, being Rutherford, he naturally put his finger upon the essential point, the release of neutrons in quantity. It was his old student of the McGill days, Otto Hahn, who two years later showed how the uranium nucleus could be split, with just such a release of neutrons, a discovery which, together with Fermi's work, was to lead in the course of a few years to the atomic bomb. In connection with this terrible consequence of his own work on the nucleus another utterance of Rutherford's at about the same time seems appropriate: "I am doubtful, however, whether the most imaginative scientific man, except in rare cases, is able to foresee the result of any discovery."

A characteristic of his genius was that Rutherford seemed to know by instinct what observations were important and what were relatively trivial. Many people seem to think that great scientific discoveries are due to stringent sequences of logical thought, leading inexorably from one conclusion to another. They are more often due to some chance observation, recognized as significant by a kind of instinct, following on long and intense preoccupation with a particular subject. The famous German professor Friedrich Wilhelm Kohlrausch said of [English chemist and physicist Michael] Faraday, "He smells the truth," and the same might be said of Rutherford. The fact that a few alpha particles were observed to be scattered through an unexpectedly large angle might have been some triviality, might have been a spurious effect due to some chance radioactive contamination. Anyhow the scattering of alpha particles might not have been a matter that deserved prolonged attention. Rutherford saw that the large-angle scattering was of profound importance and, as a result of always having the subject in his mind, conceived the nuclear structure of the atom.

Isaac Newton, when asked how he made his discoveries, said, "By always thinking unto them," and, on another occasion, "I keep the subject constantly before me and wait until the first dawnings open little by little into the full light." Rutherford was in character and personality totally unlike Newton, but he could have said the same thing. . . .

A massive simplicity, an unsophisticated greatness characterized the man, whose name will endure as long as our civilization lasts. Referring to his odes, the poet Horace wrote, *Exegi monumentum aere perennius*—I have erected a monument which will last longer than bronze. Rutherford could have said the same of his work.

A Survivor Tells of the Ordeal

by Lawrence Beesley

Lawrence Beesley was on board the *Titanic*, heading to the United States for a vacation in 1912. His account of the sinking powerfully portrays what it was like for a passenger that fateful April night. Beesley describes below the first time he was aware that something was wrong with the ship, the reactions of various passengers, the use of the lifeboats, and the final view of the stricken ship.

The *Titanic* was a British ocean liner that planned to sail from England to New York City on its maiden voyage in April 1912. On the night of April 14 it struck an iceberg and sank about sixteen hundred miles from its destination. Experts had considered the ship unsinkable, but the collision sliced its hull open under water. After about two-and-a-half hours, the ship sank, causing the death of approximately fifteen hundred passengers.

And then, as I read in the quietness of the night, broken only by the muffled sound that came to me through the ventilators of stewards talking and moving along the corridors, when nearly all the passengers were in their cabins, some asleep in bed, others undressing, and others only just down from the smoking-room and still discussing many things, there came what seemed to me nothing more than an extra heave of the engines and a more than usually obvious dancing motion of the mattress on which I sat. Nothing more than that—no sound of a crash or of anything else: no sense of shock, no jar that felt like one heavy body meeting another. And presently the same thing

Lawrence Beesley, "The Loss of the S.S. 'Titanic,'" *The Story of the Titanic*, edited by Jack Winocour. New York: Dover Publications, Inc., 1960. Copyright © 1960 by Dover Publications, Inc. Reproduced by permission.

repeated with about the same intensity. The thought came to me that they must have still further increased the speed. And all this time the *Titanic* was being cut open by the iceberg and water was pouring in her side, and yet no evidence that would indicate such a disaster had been presented to us. It fills me with astonishment now to think of it. Consider the question of list alone. Here was this enormous vessel running starboard-side onto an iceberg, and a passenger sitting quietly in bed, reading, felt no motion or list to the opposite or port side, and this must have been felt had it been more than the usual roll of the ship—never very much in the calm weather we had all the way. Again, my bunk was fixed to the wall on the starboard side, and any list to port would have tended to fling me out on the floor: I am sure I should have noted it had there been any. And yet the explanation is simple enough: the *Titanic* struck the berg with a force of impact of over a million foot-tons; her plates were less than an inch thick, and they must have been cut through as a knife cuts paper: there would be no need to list; it would have been better if she had listed and thrown us out on the floor, for it would have been an indication that our plates were strong enough to offer, at any rate, some resistance to the blow, and we might all have been safe to-day.

And so, with no thought of anything serious having happened to the ship, I continued my reading; and still the murmur from the stewards and from adjoining cabins, and no other sound: no cry in the night; no alarm given; no one afraid—there was then nothing which could cause fear to the most timid person. But in a few moments I felt the engines slow and stop; the dancing motion and the vibration ceased suddenly after being part of our very existence for four days, and that was the first hint that anything out of the ordinary had happened. . . .

First Reactions

Like a flash it came to me: "We have dropped a propeller blade: when this happens the engines always race away until they are controlled, and this accounts for the extra heave they gave"; not a very logical conclusion when considered now, for the engines should have continued to heave all the time until we stopped, but it was at the time a sufficiently tenable hypothesis to hold. Acting on it, I jumped out of bed, slipped on a dressing-gown over pajamas, put on shoes, and went out of my cabin into the hall near the saloon. Here was a steward leaning against the staircase, probably waiting until those in the smoke-room above had gone to bed and he could put out the lights. I said, "Why have we stopped?" "I don't know, sir," he replied, "but I don't suppose it is anything much." "Well," I said, "I am going on deck to see what it is," and started towards the stairs. He smiled indulgently at me as I passed him, and said, "All right, sir, but it is mighty cold up there." I am sure at that time he thought I was rather foolish to go up with so little reason, and I must confess I felt rather absurd for not remaining in the cabin: it seemed like making a needless fuss to walk about the ship in a dressing-gown. But it was my first trip across the sea, I had enjoyed every minute of it and was keenly alive to note every new experience; and certainly to stop in the middle of the sea with a propeller dropped seemed sufficient reason for going on deck. And yet the steward, with his fatherly smile, and the fact that no one else was about the passages or going upstairs to reconnoiter, made me feel guilty in an undefined way or breaking some code of a ship's régime—an Englishman's fear of being thought "unusual," perhaps!

I climbed the three flights of stairs, opened the vestibule door leading to the top deck, and stepped out into an atmosphere that cut me, clad as I was, like a knife. Walking to the starboard side, I peered over and saw the sea many feet below, calm and black; forward, the deserted deck stretching away to the first-class quarters and the captain's bridge; and behind, the steerage quarters and the stern bridge; nothing more: no iceberg on either side or astern as far as we could see in the darkness. There were two or three men on deck, and with one—the Scotch engineer who played hymns in the saloon—I compared notes of our experiences. He had just begun to undress when the engines stopped and had come up at once, so that he was fairly well-clad; none of us could see anything, and all being quiet and still, the Scotchman and I went down to the next deck. Through the windows of the smoking-room we saw a game of cards going on, with several onlookers, and went in to enquire if they knew more than we did. They had apparently felt rather more of the heaving motion, but so far as I remember, none of them had gone out on deck to make any enquiries, even when one of them had seen through the windows an iceberg go by towering above the decks. He had called their attention to it, and they all watched it disappear, but had then at once resumed the game. We asked them the height of the berg and some said one hundred feet, others, sixty feet; one of the onlookers—a motor engineer traveling to America with a model carbureter (he had filled in his declaration form near me in the afternoon and had questioned the library steward how he should declare his patent)—said, "Well, I am accustomed to estimating distances and I put it at between eighty and ninety feet." We accepted his estimate and made guesses as to what had happened to the *Titanic*: the general impression was that we had just scraped the iceberg with a glancing blow on the starboard side, and they had stopped as a wise precaution, to examine her thoroughly all over. "I expect the iceberg has scratched off some of her new paint," said one, "and the captain doesn't like to go on until she is painted up again." We laughed at his estimate of the captain's care for the ship. Poor Captain Smith!—he knew by this time only too well what had happened.

One of the players, pointing to his glass of whiskey standing at his elbow, and turning to an onlooker, said, "Just run along the deck and see if any ice has come aboard: I would like some for this." Amid the general laughter at what we thought was his imagination—only too realistic, alas! for when he spoke the forward deck was covered with ice that had tumbled over—and seeing that no more information was forthcoming, I left the smoking-room and went down to my cabin, where I sat for some time reading again. I am filled with sorrow to think I never saw any of the occupants of that smoking-room again: nearly all young men full of hope for their prospects in a new world; mostly unmarried; keen, alert, with the makings of good citizens. Presently, hearing people walking about the corridors, I looked out and saw several standing in the hall talking to a steward—most of them ladies in dressing-gowns; other people were going upstairs, and I decided to go on deck again, but as it was too cold to do so in a dressing-gown, I dressed in a Norfolk jacket and trousers and walked up. There were now more people looking over the side and walking about, questioning each other as to why we had stopped, but without obtaining any definite information. I stayed on deck some minutes, walking about vigorously to keep warm and occasionally looking downwards to the sea as if something there would indicate the reason for delay. The ship had now resumed her course, moving very slowly through the water with a little white line of foam on each side. I think we were all glad to see this: it seemed better than standing still. I soon decided to go down again, and as I crossed from the starboard to the port side to go down by the vestibule door, I saw an officer climb on the last lifeboat on the port side—number 16—and begin to throw off the cover, but I do not remember that any one paid any particular attention to him. Certainly no one thought they were preparing to man the lifeboats and embark from the ship. All this time there was no apprehension of any danger in the minds of passengers, and no one was in any condition of panic or hysteria; after all, it would have been strange if they had been, without any definite evidence of danger.

As I passed to the door to go down, I looked forward again and saw to my surprise an undoubted tilt downwards from the stern to the bows: only a slight slope, which I don't think any one had noticed—at any rate, they had not remarked on it. As I went downstairs a confirmation of this tilting forward came in something unusual about the stairs, a curious sense of something out of balance and of not being able to put one's feet down in the right place. . . .

I left . . . and went again to my cabin. I put on some underclothing, sat on the sofa, and read for some ten minutes, when I heard through the open door, above, the noise of people passing up and down, and a loud shout from above: "All passengers on deck with lifebelts on.". . .

On Deck

Reaching the top deck, we found many people assembled there—some fully dressed, with coats and wraps, well-prepared for anything that might happen; others who had thrown wraps hastily round them when they were called or heard the summons to equip themselves with lifebelts—not in much condition to face the cold of that night. Fortunately there was no wind to beat the cold air through our clothing: even the breeze caused by the ship's motion had died entirely away, for the engines had stopped again and the *Titanic* lay peacefully on the surface of the sea—motionless, quiet, not even rocking to the roll of the sea; indeed, as we were to discover presently, the sea was as calm as an inland lake save for the gentle swell which could impart no motion to a ship the size of the *Titanic*. To stand on the deck many feet above the water lapping idly against her sides, and looking much farther off than it really was because of the darkness, gave one a sense of wonderful security: to feel her so steady and still was like standing on a large rock in the middle of the ocean. But there were now more evidences of the coming catastrophe to the observer than had been apparent when on deck last: one was the roar and hiss of escaping steam from the boilers, issuing out of a large steam pipe reaching high up one of the funnels: a harsh, deafening boom that made conversation difficult and no doubt increased the apprehension of some people merely because of the volume of noise. . . .

From the time we came on deck until boat 13 got away, I heard very little conversation of any kind among the passengers. It is not the slightest exaggeration to say that no signs of alarm were exhibited by any one: there was no indication of panic or hysteria; no cries of fear, and no running to and fro to discover what was the matter, why we had been summoned on deck with lifebelts, and what was to be done with us now we were there. We stood there quietly looking on at the work of the crew as they manned the lifeboats, and no one ventured to interfere with them or offered to help them. It was plain we should be of no use; and the crowd of men and women stood quietly on the deck or paced slowly up and down waiting for orders from the officers. . . .

I was now on the starboard side of the top boat deck; the time about 12.20. We watched the crew at work on the lifeboats, numbers 9, 11, 13, 15, some inside arranging the oars, some coiling ropes on the deck—the ropes which ran through the pulleys to lower to the sea—others with cranks fitted to the rocking arms of the davits. As we watched, the cranks were turned, the davits swung outwards until the boats hung clear of the edge of the deck. Just then an officer came along from the first-class deck and shouted above the noise of escaping steam, "All women and children get down to deck below and all men stand back from the boats.". . .

But if there were any one who had not by now realized that the ship was in danger, all doubt on this point was to be set at rest in a dramatic manner. Suddenly a rush of light from the forward deck, a hissing roar that made us all turn from watching the boats, and a rocket leapt upwards to where the stars blinked and twinkled above us. Up it went, higher and higher, with a sea of faces upturned to watch it, and then an explosion that seemed to split the silent night in two, and a shower of stars sank slowly down and went out one by one. And with a gasping sigh one word escaped the lips of the crowd: "Rockets!" Anybody knows what rockets at sea mean. And presently another, and then a third. It is no use denying the dramatic intensity of the scene: separate it if you can from all the terrible events that followed, and picture the calmness of the night, the sudden light on the decks crowded with people in different stages of dress and undress, the background of huge funnels and tapering masts revealed by the soaring rocket, whose flash illumined at the same time the faces and minds of the obedient crowd, the one with mere physical light, the other with a sudden revelation of what its message was. Every one knew without being told that we were calling for help from any one who was near enough to see.

The crew were now in the boats, the sailors standing by the pulley ropes let them slip through the cleats in jerks, and down the boats went till level with B deck; women and children climbed over the rail into the boats and filled them; when full, they were lowered one by one, beginning with number 9, the first on the second-class deck, and working backwards towards 15. All this we could see by peering over the edge of the boat-deck, which was now quite open to the sea, the four boats which formed a natural barrier being lowered from the deck and leaving it exposed. . . .

Soon after the men had left the starboard side, I saw a bandsman—the 'cellist—come round the vestibule corner from the staircase entrance and run down the now deserted starboard deck, his 'cello trailing behind him, the spike dragging along the floor. This must have been about 12.40 A.M. I suppose the band must have begun to play soon after this and gone on until after 2 A.M. Many brave things were done that night, but none more brave than by those few men playing minute after minute as the ship settled quietly lower and lower in the sea and the sea rose higher and higher to where they stood; the music they played serving alike as their own immortal requiem and their right to be recorded on the rolls of undying fame.

Looking forward and downward, we could see several of the boats now in the water, moving slowly one by one from the side, without confusion or noise, and stealing away in the darkness which swallowed them in turn as the crew bent to the oars. . . .

Almost immediately after this, I heard a cry from below of, "Any more ladies?" and looking over the edge of the deck, saw boat 13 swinging level with the rail of B deck, with the crew, some stokers, a few men passengers and the rest ladies—the latter being about half the total number; the boat was almost full and just about to be lowered. The call for ladies was repeated twice again, but apparently there were none to be found. Just then one of the crew looked up and saw me looking over. "Any ladies on your deck?" he said. "No," I replied. "Then you had better jump." I sat on the edge of the deck with my feet over, threw the dressing-gown (which I had carried on my arm all of the time) into the boat, dropped, and fell in the boat near the stern. . . .

In the Lifeboat

It certainly was thrilling to see the black hull of the ship on one side and the sea, seventy feet below, on the other, or to pass down by cabins and saloons brilliantly lighted; but we knew nothing of the apprehension felt in the minds of some of the officers whether the boats and lowering-gear would stand the strain of the weight of our sixty people. The ropes, however, were new and strong, and the boat did not buckle in the middle as an older boat might have done. Whether it was right or not to lower boats full of people to the water—and it seems likely it was not—I think there can be nothing but the highest praise given to the officers and crew above for the way in which they lowered the boats one after the other safely to the water; it may seem a simple matter, to read about such a thing, but any sailor knows, apparently, that it is not so. An experienced officer has told me that he has seen a boat lowered in practise from a ship's deck, with a trained crew and no passengers in the boat, with practised sailors paying out the ropes, in daylight, in calm weather, with the ship lying in dock—and has seen the boat tilt over and pitch the crew headlong into the sea. Contrast these conditions with those obtaining that Monday morning at 12.45 A.M., and it is impossible not to feel that, whether the lowering crew were trained or not, whether they had or had not drilled since coming on board, they did their duty in a way that argues the greatest efficiency. I cannot help feeling the deepest gratitude to the two sailors who stood at the ropes above and lowered us to the sea: I do not suppose they were saved. . . .

We had no eyes for anything but the ship we had just left. As the oarsmen pulled slowly away we all turned and took a long look at the mighty vessel towering high above our midget boat, and I know it must have been the most extraordinary sight I shall ever be called upon to witness; I realize now how totally inadequate language is to convey to some other person who was not there any real impression of what we saw.

But the task must be attempted: the whole picture is so intensely dramatic that, while it is not possible to place on paper for eyes to see the actual likeness of the ship as she lay there, some sketch of the scene will be possible. First of all, the climatic conditions were extraordinary. The night was one of the most beautiful I have ever seen: the sky without a single cloud to mar the perfect brilliance of the stars, clustered so thickly together that in places there seemed almost more dazzling points of light set in the black sky than background of sky itself; and each star seemed, in the keen atmosphere, free from any haze, to have increased its brilliance tenfold and to twinkle and glitter with a staccato flash that made the sky seem nothing but a setting made for them in which to display their wonder. They seemed so near, and their light so much more intense than ever before, that fancy suggested they saw this beautiful ship in dire distress below and all their energies had awakened to flash messages across the black dome of the sky to each other; telling and warning of the calamity happening in the world beneath. . . .

And next the cold air! Here again was something quite new to us: there was not a breath of wind to blow keenly round us as we stood in the boat, and because of its continued persistence to make us feel cold; it was just a keen, bitter, icy, motionless cold that came from nowhere and yet was there all the time; the stillness of it—if one can imagine "cold" being motionless and still—was what seemed new and strange.

And these—the sky and the air—were overhead; and below was the sea. Here again something uncommon: the surface was like a lake of oil, heaving gently up and down with a quiet motion that rocked our boat dreamily to and fro. We did not need to keep her head to the swell: often I watched her lying broadside on to the tide, and with a boat loaded as we were, this would have been impossible with anything like a swell. The sea slipped away smoothly under the boat, and I think we never heard it lapping on the sides, so oily in appearance was the water. . . .

A Last Look

And so in these conditions of sky and air and sea, we gazed broadside on the *Titanic* from a short distance. She was absolutely still—indeed from the first it seemed as if the blow from the iceberg had taken all the courage out of her and she had just come quietly to rest and was settling down without an effort to save herself, without a murmur of protest against such a foul blow. For the sea could not rock her: the wind was not there to howl noisily round the decks, and make the ropes hum; from the first what must have impressed all as they watched was the sense of stillness about her and the slow, insensible way she sank lower and lower in the sea, like a stricken animal.

The mere bulk alone of the ship viewed from the sea below was an awe-inspiring sight. Imagine a ship nearly a sixth of a mile long, 75 feet high to the top decks, with four enormous funnels above the decks, and masts again high above the funnels; with her hundreds of portholes, all her saloons and other rooms brilliant with light, and all round her, little boats filled with those who until a few hours before had trod her decks and read in her libraries and listened to the music of her band in happy content; and who were now looking up in amazement at the enormous mass above them and rowing away from her because she was sinking. . . .

And one other thing was different from expectation: the thing that ripped away from us instantly, as we saw it, all sense of the beauty of the night, the beauty of the ship's lines, and the beauty of her lights—and all these taken in themselves were intensely beautiful—that thing was the awful angle made by the level of the sea with the rows of porthole lights along her side in dotted lines, row above row. The sea level and the rows of lights should have been parallel—should never have met—and now they met at an angle inside the black hull of the ship. There was nothing else to indicate she was injured; nothing but this apparent violation of a simple geometrical law—that parallel lines should "never meet even if produced ever so far both ways"; but it meant the *Titanic* had sunk by the head until the lowest portholes in the bows were under the sea, and the portholes in the stern were lifted above the normal height. We rowed away from her in the quietness of the night, hoping and praying with all our hearts that she would sink no more and the day would find her still in the same position as she was then. The crew, however, did not think so. It has been said frequently that the officers and crew felt assured that she would remain afloat even after they knew the extent of the damage. Some of them may have done so—and perhaps, from their scientific knowledge of her construction, with more reason at the time than those who said she would sink— but at any rate the stokers in our boat had no such illusion. One of them—I think he was the same man that cut us free from the pulley ropes—told us how he was at work in the stoke-hole, and in anticipation of going off duty in quarter of an hour—thus confirming the time of the collision as 11.45—had near him a pan of soup keeping hot on some part of the machinery; suddenly the whole side of the compartment came in, and the water rushed him off his feet. Picking himself up, he sprang for the compartment doorway and was just through the aperture when the watertight door came down behind him, "like a knife," as he said, "they work them from the bridge.". . .

The Sinking

And all the time, as we watched, the *Titanic* sank lower and lower by the head and the angle became wider and wider as the stern porthole lights lifted and the bow lights sank, and it was evident she was not to stay afloat much longer. The captain-stoker now told the oarsmen to row away as hard as they could. Two reasons seemed to make this a wise decision: one that as she sank she would create such a wave of suction that boats, if not sucked under by being too near, would be in danger of being swamped by the wave her sinking would create—and we all knew our boat was in no condition to ride big waves, crowded as it was and manned with untrained oarsmen. The second was that an explosion might result from the water getting to the boilers, and débris might fall within a wide radius. And yet, as it turned out, neither of these things happened.

At about 2.15 A.M. I think we were any distance from a mile to two miles away. It is difficult for a landsman to calculate distance at sea but we had been afloat an hour and a half, the boat was heavily loaded, the oarsmen unskilled, and our course erratic: following now one light and now another, sometimes a star and sometimes a light from a port lifeboat which had turned away from the *Titanic* in the opposite direction and lay almost on our horizon; and so we could not have gone very far away.

About this time, the water had crept up almost to her sidelight and the captain's bridge, and it seemed a question only of minutes before she sank. The oarsmen lay on their oars, and all in the lifeboat were motionless as we watched her in absolute silence—save some who would not look and buried their heads on each other's shoulders. The lights still shone with the same brilliance, but not so many of them: many were now below the surface. I have often wondered since whether they continued to light up the cabins when the portholes were under water; they may have done so.

And then, as we gazed awe-struck, she tilted slowly up, revolving apparently about a center of gravity just astern of amidships, until she attained a vertically upright position; and there she remained—motionless! As she swung up, her lights, which had shone without a flicker all night, went out suddenly, came on again for a single flash, then went out altogether. And as they did so, there came a noise which many people, wrongly I think, have described as an explosion; it has always seemed to me that it was nothing but the engines and machinery coming loose from their bolts and bearings, and falling through the compartments, smashing everything in their way. It was partly a roar, partly a groan, partly a rattle, and partly a smash, and it was not a sudden roar as an explosion would be: it went on successively for some seconds, possibly fifteen to twenty, as the heavy machinery dropped down to the bottom (now the bows) of the ship: I suppose it fell through the end and sank first, before the ship. But it was a noise no one had heard before, and no one wishes to hear again: it was stupefying, stupendous, as it came to us along the water. It was as if all the heavy things one could think of had been thrown downstairs from the top of a house, smashing each other and the stairs and everything in the way.

Several apparently authentic accounts have been given, in which definite stories of explosions have been related—in some cases even with wreckage blown up and the ship broken in two; but I think such accounts will not stand close analysis. In the first place the fires had been withdrawn and the steam allowed to escape some time before she sank, and the possibility of explosion from this cause seems very remote. Then, as just related, the noise was not sudden and definite, but prolonged—more like the roll and crash of thunder. . . . As the *Titanic* tilted up [the engines] would almost certainly fall loose from their bed and plunge down through the other compartments.

No phenomenon like that pictured in some American and English papers occurred—that of the ship breaking in two, and the two ends being raised above the surface. I saw these drawings in preparation on board the *Carpathia*, and said at the time that they bore no resemblance to what actually happened.

When the noise was over the *Titanic* was still upright like a column: we could see her now only as the stern and some 150 feet of her stood outlined against the star-specked sky, looming black in the darkness, and in this position she continued for some minutes—I think as much as five minutes, but it may have been less.

Then, first sinking back a little at the stern, I thought, she slid slowly forwards through the water and dived slantingly down; the sea closed over her and we had seen the last of the beautiful ship on which we had embarked four days before at Southampton.

And in place of the ship on which all our interest had been concentrated for so long and towards which we looked most of the time because it was still the only object on the sea which was a fixed point to us—in place of the *Titanic*, we had the level sea now stretching in an unbroken expanse to the horizon: heaving gently just as before, with no indication on the surface that the waves had just closed over the most wonderful vessel ever built by man's hand; the stars looked down just the same and the air was just as bitterly cold.

There seemed a great sense of loneliness when we were left on the sea in a small boat without the *Titanic*: not that we were uncomfortable (except for the cold) nor in danger: we did not think we were either, but the *Titanic* was no longer there.

We waited head on for the wave which we thought might come—the wave we had heard so much of from the crew and which they said had been known to travel for miles—and it never came. But although the *Titanic* left us no such legacy of a wave as she went to the bottom, she left us something we would willingly forget forever, something which it is well not to let the imagination dwell on—the cries of many hundreds of our fellow-passengers struggling in the ice-cold water.

I would willingly omit any further mention of this part of the disaster from this book, but for two reasons it is not possible—first, that as a matter of history it should be put on record; and secondly, that these cries were not only an appeal for help in the awful conditions of danger in which the drowning found themselves—an appeal that could never be answered—but an appeal to the whole world to make such conditions of danger and hopelessness impossible ever again; a cry that called to the heavens for the very injustice of its own existence: a cry that clamored for its own destruction.

We were utterly surprised to hear this cry go up as the waves closed over the *Titanic*: we had heard no sound of any kind from her since we left her side; and, as mentioned before, we did not know how many boats she had or how many rafts. The crew may have known, but they probably did not, and if they did, they never told the passengers: we should not have been surprised to know all were safe on some life-saving device.

So that unprepared as we were for such a thing, the cries of the drowning floating across the quiet sea filled us with stupefaction: we longed to return and rescue at least some of the drowning, but we knew it was impossible. The boat was filled to standing-room, and to return would mean the swamping of us all, and so the captain-stoker told his crew to row away from the cries. We tried to sing to keep all from thinking of them; but there was no heart for singing in the boat at that time.

The cries, which were loud and numerous at first, died away gradually one by one, but the night was clear, frosty and still, the water smooth, and the sounds must have carried on its level surface free from any obstruction for miles, certainly much farther from the ship than we were situated. I think the last of them must have been heard nearly forty minutes after the *Titanic* sank. Lifebelts would keep the survivors afloat for hours; but the cold water was what stopped the cries.

There must have come to all those safe in the lifeboats, scattered round the drowning at various distances, a deep resolve that, if anything could be done by them in the future to prevent the repetition of such sounds, they would do it—at whatever cost of time or other things. And not only to them are those cries an imperative call, but to every man and woman who has known of them. It is not possible that ever again can such conditions exist; but it is a duty imperative on one and all to see that they do not. Think of it! a few more boats, a few more planks of wood nailed together in a particular way at a trifling cost, and all those men and women whom the world can so ill afford to lose would be with us to-day, there would be no mourning in thousands of homes which now are desolate, and these words need not have been written.

The *Titanic* Tragedy Has Widespread Consequences

by Paul Heyer

Almost all events from the year 1912 have faded from memory. But the story of the *Titanic* has continued to exert a powerful hold over people's imaginations. It was a symbol of its time. Its status, level of technology, and luxurious accommodations made it a perfect representative of the early 1900s Western civilization before the terrible fighting of World War I cast a pall over the earlier prewar optimism.

There were many tangible results of this tragedy. Paul Heyer, a professor of communication at Simon Fraser University, discusses in the following portions of his book what some of these were. He explains the increase in the power of the media, new maritime regulations that took effect after the disaster, and the rise of the *New York Times* were direct results of the terrible event. Finally, he offers an intriguing look at the *Titanic* as myth, which may help account for its enduring appeal.

T he sinking of the *Titanic* is our century's first collective nightmare. The confused and anguished response it provoked—culture shock is the term that comes to mind—can be seen as a harbinger of reactions that would follow Hiroshima, the Holocaust, JFK's assassination, and most recently, the Oklahoma City bombing.

Since the bewildering events of 1912, the ship has never strayed far from media concern. In 1985, the discovery of the wreck attracted worldwide attention. A year later, the *Challenger* explosion repeated the *Titanic*'s lesson of technological hubris. . . .

More than just a tragedy entailing great loss of life, the sinking of the *Titanic* endures as our century's most persistent reminder of the danger in underestimating nature and overestimating technology. . . .

In various ways, [the sinking of the *Titanic*] relates to all the media. . . . Her initial circumstances were brought to public awareness through a dynamic web of information movement whose strands included the telegraph, telephone, wireless, and popular press. Her fate has been dramatized and analyzed on radio and television and in film.

The story of the *Titanic* also presents us with elements that are more difficult to assess—and access. In addition to being one of this century's major news stories, it has become a mystery and a myth of unparalleled enormity. It remains a mystery how and why, at almost full speed on the clearest of evenings, the "unsinkable" *Titanic* met the iceberg that authored its doom; as myth, the *Titanic* shares with the *Challenger* the capacity to derive a moral lesson from technological failure.

Why are we so fascinated by a disaster that throughout our century has been frequently surpassed by others in terms of loss of life? Partial explanations have been occasionally attempted. Most deal with the moral implications of the story—technological arrogance leading to a disregard for the forces of nature, the rich and famous paying with their lives, and the disaster as a finale for one era and overture to the next.

Explaining the meaning of the *Titanic*, however, entails not just analyzing the way her fate evokes literary notions of the tragic. It necessitates appraising the cultural and technological circumstances in which the drama has been, and is still being, played out. Using what can perhaps be described as the "archival archaeology" of a variety of media, we can then begin the task of unraveling the *Titanic*'s greatest mystery and central theme of subsequent chapters: not why she struck an iceberg on a cold April night once-upon-a-time, but the hold the event still has over us. . . .

Wireless Communication and the Sinking

Prior to the *Titanic* disaster and especially during the first decade
of wireless, seamen put supreme trust in the visual verification
of phenomena. Wireless messages about a hazard such as icebergs were often less a call to action than a call to greater vigi-
lance. Given the presence of ice in her route, the *Titanic* could
have slowed down or changed to a more southerly course and
even speeded up. She did neither, but preferred to wait and *see*
before acting. This suggests that prior to the sinking, when large
companies like the White Star Line routed their vessels, wireless
played a supplemental rather than a determining role. . . .

The sinking of the *Titanic* demonstrated that nothing in the
realm of transportation and communication could or should be
taken for granted. Wireless was now deemed indispensable and
in need of regulatory policies appropriate to the role it played in
the movement of information and people. Previously, attitudes
about how to control the new medium had been ambivalent.

In the years leading up to the *Titanic* disaster, the general public regarded wireless with a mixture of awe and indifference. It
was awesome when a heart-stopping event, such as the sinking
of the *Republic* [a luxury liner that struck another vessel and sank
in 1909], thrust the technology and those associated with it into
the media spotlight. Apart from these visible moments, in its normal day-to-day, year-to-year operations, wireless was often taken
for granted. Although Marconi was widely known, the success
of his commercial ventures only occasionally equaled the renown
of his name. Not until 1910 would his empire be solidly in the
black to stay.

During this early period there was little call for regulation on
the part of the press. Most newspapers seemed content to wait for
the next wireless event or hero. While the sinking of the *Titanic*
inherited this expectation, it did so with a difference, particularly
when news broke about the inaction of the *Californian* [a ship that
was close to the *Titanic* at the time of the sinking]. On one hand,
the press regarded wireless as having performed up to all previous expectations; on the other, it suggested that with better mon-
itoring the medium might have helped save more lives. . . .

The initial public response to the role of wireless in the disaster
was largely positive. Marconi, along with the *Titanic*'s deceased
operator, Jack Phillips, were given heroic treatment in the press at
a time when heroes were sorely needed. The sentiments expressed

in a speech by the British postmaster general on 18 April summed up the attitude of many people on both sides of the Atlantic (with the possible exception of Senator Smith): "Those who had been saved had been saved by one man—Mr. Marconi." Among the American accolades was a telegram from Thomas Edison, who had publicly endorsed Marconi's abilities a few years earlier.

To be celebrated in this way was perhaps the high point of Marconi's career. The invention that for over a decade had been linked to his name was now synonymous with it. Unprecedented business opportunities followed. . . .

The call for wireless regulation in the press and at the two inquiries, was more tempered than the one dealing with shipping and navigational practice. In the latter arena, outrage was expressed over the frequent practice of large liners, with fewer lifeboat spaces than passengers, steaming rapidly at night through regions where ice was present. Here, the White Star Line was chastised for doing what was often done by other companies.

In the wake of Senator Smith's inquiry, the U.S. government had no intention of waiting over a year for a new international wireless convention to make policy changes. In July, President Taft signed into law an amendment to the 1910 Wireless Ship Act. Vessels covered by the original act described earlier now had to have two operators on duty so the station could function twenty-four hours a day, and an auxiliary power source. Also in July, a sweeping bill was passed, the Radio Act, which became law the following December. . . .

The Radio Act established new procedures for distress calls, in part to prevent the type of confusion that plagued some of the *Titanic*'s last transmissions. A distress frequency was established, and when it was being used all ships and shore stations unable to assist directly or relay the message were to cease signaling. In addition, shore stations had to monitor this frequency every fifteen minutes for two minutes. SOS was deemed to be the official distress call. . . .

The quick action on the part of American legislators following the *Titanic* disaster influenced the proceedings of the International Conference for the Safety of Life at Sea held in London between 12 November 1913 and 20 January 1914. Policies were implemented affecting lifeboats, navigational procedures in hazardous conditions, the establishment of an international ice patrol, and communications. . . .

Since the *Titanic* perished in 1912, no oceangoing vessel using the Atlantic shipping lanes has been lost because of a collision with ice. The London Conference unequivocally showed that maritime communication had come a long way from the kind of incident that befell the Collins liner *Pacific* in 1856: months after she disappeared without a trace, a message in a bottle drifted to the Hebrides. It described the ship going down surrounded by icebergs. . . .

The Rise of the *New York Times*

Reporting the story of the *Titanic* would involve all three representatives of the original penny press and a *Times* that had been reborn in 1896 when Adolph Ochs took over. It would also pose a major journalistic challenge for the two papers that actually led the city in circulation in 1912, Pulitzer's *New York World* and Hearst's *New York Journal*. . . .

The first wireless reports stating the *Titanic* had struck an iceberg, was sinking by the bow, and putting women into lifeboats, reached newsrooms in the early morning hours of 15 April. Available information also indicated that several ships were rapidly steaming to her aid. Around these "facts," and a number of additional sketchy and sometimes conflicting messages, stories had to be written. With so few details, interpretation necessarily augmented reporting. . . .

The tenor of the coverage ranged from the *Times*'s somber assemblage of evidence suggesting the worst to the imprudently optimistic exhortations of the *Journal*.

The *Times* account listed the known facts in an extended headline: "NEW LINER TITANIC HITS ICEBERG; SINKING BY THE BOW AT MIDNIGHT; WOMEN PUT OFF IN LIFE BOATS; LAST WIRELESS AT 12:27 A.M. BLURRED." The ominous follow-up text noted how the wireless transmissions ended abruptly and that the *Virginian* and *Baltic* were attempting to go to the *Titanic*'s position. . . .

The reserved *Tribune* ran most of the same information on its front page, but emphasized the "reassuring feature" that considerable assistance was on the way. The *Herald* did likewise, with part of its headline reading "VESSELS RUSH TO HER SIDE.". . .

The hint of hope became a virtual promise in the *Sun* and *Journal*. Although the morning *Sun* merely reported that the *Titanic* had hit an iceberg, the headline of the evening edition read,

"TITANIC'S PASSENGERS ARE TRANSHIPPED." The sub-headline claimed a rescue by the *Carpathia* and *Parisian*, with the *Titanic* being towed to Halifax by the *Virginian*. The headline of the final edition stated, "ALL SAVED FROM TITANIC AFTER COLLISION.". . . .

Hearst's *Journal*, using the boldest headline of any paper, was even more optimistic: "ALL SAFE ON TITANIC." A box to the left contained a subheadline claiming the liner was in tow, along with a picture of the ship and her captain. Subsequent commentary posited that four vessels were involved in the rescue, which was facilitated by calm seas. . . .

When more and verifiable information regarding the *Titanic*'s plight came into New York newsrooms later on the 15th, it made the next day's edition of each paper pivotal. The cautiously pessimistic *Times* gained public confidence, while the *Sun* and *Journal* struggled to maintain a readership they had earlier misled. . . .

Within twenty-four hours the magnitude of the tragedy was acknowledged by White Star's New York office; they had earlier denied the seriousness of the situation to Van Anda [managing editor for the *New York Times*] when he inquired by telephone. The *Times* earned national and international attention for its astute coverage, as well as through the sale of some of its stories to other papers over the next several days. . . .

Not since the exposure of Boss Tweed had the paper been so high profile, and this time the visibility was international.

Several years later, when Van Anda went to London and visited the offices of Lord Northcliffe's *Daily Mail*, the editor on duty produced a copy of the renowned issue of the *Times* and said, "We keep this as an example of the greatest accomplishment in news reporting." Even today, it remains the most important single issue contributing to the establishment of the *Times* as a global voice. . . .

The tragedy was without precedent, not in the terms of loss of life but with respect to how it illustrated the unimaginable convergence of so many factors. The old adage about truth being stranger than fiction must have seemed appropriate. After the two hearings, there was a sense that the loss of the *Titanic* was not just a devastating accident whose painful memory would eventually recede but also a scar on the very soul of western civilization. One element that made it so unsettling was the way the cast of characters in the drama were deployed. Technology and nature shared the lead, with individual personalities assigned to supporting roles—a reversal of the way major historical events were usually played out. Never had [American essayist and poet Ralph Waldo] Emerson's observation the "Things are in the saddle and ride mankind" rung so true. . . .

In mid-May of 1987, I was in the Philippines traveling between Mindoro Island and Luzon Province in a small ferry. On December 21 of the same year, my memory of that passage turned from pleasant to haunting. At a Greenwich Village newsstand I picked up a copy of the *New York Times*. The headline told of a collision between the ferry, *Doña Paz*, and an oil tanker in waters I had once sailed; 1,500 were believed to have perished. I thought about that same casualty figure as it had appeared in a *Times*'s seventy-five years earlier. Later estimates would put the death toll at between 4,000 and 5,000.

Today the *Doña Paz* is largely forgotten, except in the Philippines, where litigation is still going on to compensate families affected by the tragedy. Without doubt, the fate of the *Doña Paz* has fallen victim to our short-term memory regarding third-world events. Yet, even the recent ferry disasters in Europe, which took hundreds of lives, have slipped from the recall of most of us. The *Titanic* is partly to blame. She wields the memory of her fate with a jealousy that tolerates no rivals.

Although we have learned much about the circumstances of

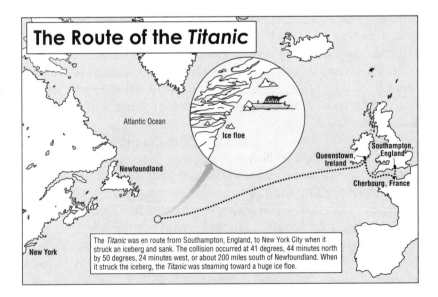

The Route of the *Titanic*

Atlantic Ocean

Ice floe

Newfoundland

Queenstown, Ireland

Southampton, England

Cherbourg, France

New York

The *Titanic* was en route from Southampton, England, to New York City when it struck an iceberg and sank. The collision occurred at 41 degrees, 44 minutes north by 50 degrees, 24 minutes west, or about 200 miles south of Newfoundland. When it struck the iceberg, the *Titanic* was steaming toward a huge ice floe.

her demise, a persistent enigma remains: Why is the tragedy still so meaningful to us? Historical facts alone cannot provide a convincing explanation. Indeed, the question itself defies closure, since the cultural circumstances in which meanings are produced and assessed constantly change. Nevertheless, the problem is worth addressing, even if the resulting answers must remain provisional and reflect a vantage point at the end of the twentieth century.

To say that the metaphoric implications of the *Titanic* disaster have given it the status of a modern myth is a contention that would probably gain acceptance among many cultural observers. But what do we mean by "myth," and how does the *Titanic* fit with our understanding of the term?

Certainly, the notion of myth as a fallacy, or inaccurate explanation for something, is inappropriate here. There is, however, another current usage of the term, which is applicable to historical events that have far-reaching implications. To illustrate it, we can use the example of a tragedy even more commented upon than the fate of the *Titanic*.

It is often said that the events surrounding the life and death of President John F. Kennedy have become a dominant myth in late twentieth-century American culture. Used in this sense, myth refers to events that represent more than the "facts" of history. It implies that the incidents referred to embody or help explain a wider set of values, beliefs, and aspirations. For example, a significant aspect of the "myth" of JFK is the notion that his death demarcates the end of a promising new direction for America; similarly, the *Titanic* disaster has often been referred to as the end of an era, or the end of a dream. . . .

Myths as a whole encompass such a wide range of phenomena that no one theory can succeed in explaining all their diverse forms and subject matter, despite the claims of practitioners. What makes the case of the *Titanic* so fascinating is that almost all major schools of myth interpretation seem to have something to offer.

If we take a sociological approach, even a non-Marxist one, class conflict emerges as a major element. The ship was a microcosm of the most profound disparities in wealth and status the era could yield. During the crisis, preferential treatment went to the wealthy in first class while many in steerage were held at bay. This situation reflected the Edwardian world view. Later commentaries would question its moral legitimacy.

This class hierarchy was, nevertheless, partly overturned by the course of events—a reversal of the natural order of things occurs frequently in myth. Despite their privilege, some notable doyens of the dollars perished. The oft-cited list includes Astor, Straus, Guggenheim, Widener, et al. This has become an enduring theme in subsequent tellings of the sinking, from "*Titanic* Toast" in African-American oral literature to Danielle Steel's recent novel *No Greater Love.* Perhaps over the decades those of us of lesser means continue to find solace in a situation where consummate affluence and extravagance—the Edwardian equivalent of "Lifestyles of the Rich and Famous"—was no assurance against Armageddon.

A psychoanalytical or psychological interpretation of the disaster would no doubt stress other elements. Freud's approach (he was fascinated by the real-life nightmare of the *Titanic*, but did not try to explain it) has a curious applicability. Playing fast and loose with it, we could say the *Titanic* disaster is a case of male culture being undone by female nature, a variation on the devouring female, or *vagina dentata* theme. Although ships are, of course, usually referred to as female (the reverse holds in French), they nonetheless represent an attempt by *Homo faber* (man the builder) to overcome the limits on his desire to conquer space imposed by the sea, the Great Mother of Waters. Add the sea's agency, an iceberg slicing away at this male creation (the "castration complex"), and the famous call "women and children first" (Nature saving her own), and the masculine is further jeopardized.

Silly? Perhaps. But an end-of-century ecological message can be culled from this interpretation. I will return to it in concluding.

In contrast to a Freudian approach, a Jungian one would perhaps see the *Titanic* disaster as a manifestation of humankind's overbearing urge to dominate nature. Unchecked reason and technology, Jung often argued, have created a dangerous split between the human and natural worlds that can render us vulnerable to disasters of our own making—the H-bomb was his primary example. Perhaps the *Titanic*'s fate, as myth, warns us of these tendencies, its effectiveness being dramatized by the ship's status as an archetypal vessel. This status suggests a symbolic womb capable of delivering a precious human cargo while being subject to suicidal tendencies that result from a false belief that nature has been mastered.

One of the most intriguing and recent approaches to myth interpretation derives from the intellectual tradition known as structuralism. . . .

The first prerequisite of a structural analysis of myth is to draw out the episodes that make up the story. This enterprise is, of course, subject to the bias of the researcher and could be somewhat arbitrary. Nevertheless, taking the *Titanic* disaster and breaking it down into its familiar and persistent themes, we get the following:

1. Largest ship ever built embarks on her maiden voyage.
2. She accommodates all social classes and has state-of-the-art aesthetic and technological appointments.
3. Ignoring ice warnings, an attempt is made to set a speed record (the latter, although not true, is widely believed, therefore part of the myth).
4. There is a collision with an iceberg.
5. Women and children are given priority during sinking.
6. The rich and famous perish.
7. Nearby ship fails to come to the rescue.

Using a degree of imagination—critics of structuralism have argued that the approach is all imagination—we can posit that the central element on the list, number 4, is the important and pivotal one. It dramatizes the opposition between nature and culture. Numbers 1–3 assume the triumph of culture over the limitations of nature, and 5–7 dramatize the consequences of that assumption. The question as to whether culture can or should attempt to triumph over nature is thus answered in the negative.

Events in a myth . . . frequently involve the overrating of something and the underrating of something else. Applying this to our story, we can posit an overrating of size, speed, wealth. What might be construed as underrated are the natural elements of weather (that calm, clear conditions posed no danger) and climate (that the time of year and presence of ice were not an overwhelming concern). Perhaps we should also add maiden voyage, since they are normally cautious affairs tinged with superstition, attitudes ignored in the instance. . . .

I would like to conclude by putting the story of the *Titanic* in this category. The sequence of events in it, rather than being totally unprecedented, can be seen as a transformation and reversal of what occurs in one of our most famous narratives: Noah's

Ark in the book of Genesis. Both stories express moral precepts by recounting a disaster involving a great ship.

According to the account in Genesis, the *Ark* was built in response to a cataclysmic flood sent by God to punish a world guilty of excessive corruption, violence, and wickedness. God's original plan was to do away with the entire enterprise, but Noah prompted him to have second thoughts. Here was a man who, in resisting what others had succumbed to, walked in a state of grace and untarnished faith.

God informed Noah of the wrath to come and instructed him to build the *Ark* of gopher wood, 300 cubits in length, 30 cubits high, and 50 cubits wide. The length of a biblical cubit has been estimated at between 18 and 36 inches. If, for the sake of poetic license, we take the latter figure and agree not to make too much of the comparison, the length of the *Ark* roughly equaled the *Titanic*'s 882 feet. Her height came close to the *Titanic*'s 97 feet from keel to boat deck. Noah's vessel, however, measured considerably broader in the beam than the *Titanic*'s 97 feet, since speed was not a high priority. God's oral blueprint also called for the *Ark* to have, like the *Titanic*, a three-tiered system of accommodations, although the *Bible* did not specify who or what went where.

Placing his faith in God and avoiding the excesses of the antediluvian era, Noah, along with his extended family and their menagerie, were spared. In the story of the *Titanic*, faith was placed in the conceits of the modern world—technology and inevitable progress. In yielding to their excesses, the ship perished.

Overweening pride, condemned in the *Bible* and in Greek tragedy (where it was labeled hubris), was the *Titanic*'s undoing. The resulting "nautical fall" recalls an earlier one in literature, whereby Captain Ahab's obsession with a white whale destroyed the *Pequod* in Melville's *Moby Dick*. And, as a case of reach exceeding grasp, the *Titanic*'s lesson appears to have been repeated less than six months after her remains were found, when the promise of the *Challenger* was immolated in January 1986.

What makes a comparison between the *Ark* and the *Titanic* so intriguing is how each vessel encapsulated the world of her day. Noah brought on board animals, crops, and a small coterie of relatives—a starter kit to rebuild civilization. The *Titanic* had impressive trappings that included a swimming pool, band, period staterooms, lavish dining areas, a café Parisien, gymnasium, squash courts, and ornate decor, all contained within a state-of-the-art, high-tech package. She was partly a grand hotel, partly a traveling exposition recalling the influential one held in Paris in 1900. In the jargon of contemporary pop culture, we could describe her as a floating theme park, part *Love Boat*, part *Fantasy Island.*

The theme of a self-sufficient world borne in the womb of a ship is a compelling one. In literature we find a renowned example in the *Nautilus*, the submarine created by Jules Verne in two of his novels, *Twenty-Thousand Leagues Under the Sea* and *The Mysterious Island. . . .*

Like the *Nautilus* and, from more recent genres of fiction, *Star Trek*'s *Enterprise*, the *Titanic* has an aura of science fiction about her. She took part of the bounty of Earth on a voyage that often seemed more imaginary than real. The trip dramatized how the limits of human achievement could be overridden by arrogance and vulnerability.

A key to understanding our enduring fascination with the outcome of that infamous maiden voyage can be found, I believe, in an observation made by several survivors in lifeboats who watched the ship's terrifying last moments. They described the scenario as "like the end of the world."

Although we tend to think of that moment as more akin to the end of an era, the way it still haunts us suggests more. Amid recent news stories of the growing crises in our biosphere resulting from our disregard for nature, and examples of technology gone awry, is a continuing interest in the *Titanic* disaster. Could not the possible destiny of our planet, "Space-Ship Earth," as Buckminster Fuller used to call it, be linked in some way to the fate of the great liner? Have not the events of April 1912 now become a global metaphor?

In Genesis, the biblical *Ark* rescued part of an ancient world from a disaster invoked by God. The *Titanic* has become an *Ark* more appropriate to the contemporary world, her fate urging us to prudence with a cautionary lesson. She warns of a possible second deluge, this one of our own making, from which no vessel can deliver us.

An Assassination Drags Europe into War

by Robert K. Massie

On June 28, 1914, Franz Ferdinand, the archduke of Austria-Hungary, was assassinated while on a visit to Sarajevo. The assassin, nineteen-year-old Gavrilo Princip, was a member of the Black Hand, a secret organization of extreme Serbian nationalists who sought independence for the south Slav provinces of the Austrian-Hungarian Empire. In the following selection, Robert K. Massie describes the fragile international situation in the months preceding the assassination, as the world seemed destined to go to war. Although the assassination itself was greeted with indifference in many parts of the world, it was the trigger that led to one of the deadliest conflagrations in human history: World War I.

[B]ritish statesman] Winston Churchill . . . on March 17, 1914 . . . spoke somberly of the situation in Europe:

The causes which might lead to a general war have not been removed and often remind us of their presence. There has not been the slightest abatement of naval and military preparation. On the contrary, we are witnessing this year increases of expenditure by Continental powers on armaments beyond all previous expenditure. The world is arming as it was never armed before. Every suggestion for arrest or limitation has so far been ineffectual.

Robert K. Massie, *Dreadnought*. New York: Random House, 1991. Copyright © 1991 by Robert K. Massie. Reproduced by permission of the publisher.

Weapons were accumulating in the armories of states harboring bitter antagonisms. France had waited forty-four years for *revanche* [revenge] and the rejoining of Alsace and Lorraine. Russia, defeated in the Far East in 1905, humiliated in the Balkans in 1908, could not afford to suffer further abasement; if another challenge were offered by Austria and Germany, it would be accepted. Austria-Hungary, facing disintegration from within, believed it could save itself by striking down the external source of its difficulties, the Kingdom of Serbia. The Hapsburg monarchy had Germany's pledge of support. Germans were ready for war. Britain's gradual adherence to the Triple Entente made more real the [German] nightmare of Encirclement. Britain, for the moment distracted by Ireland, had fears in Europe—primarily of the German Fleet—but few antagonisms. Indeed, her traditional antagonisms with France and Russia had been resolved. Whether, or for what reasons, Britain would fight remained unclear.

In Churchill's words, "the vials of wrath were full."

"I shall not live to see the world war," Bismarck said to [German shipping magnate Albert] Ballin in 1891, "but you will. And it will start in the East."

A Tottering Empire

By the summer of 1914, the Austro-Hungarian Empire had shrunk from the days of Hapsburg magnificence, but it still was larger than any Continental power except Russia. The lands ruled by the Emperor Franz Josef were a patchwork of provinces, races, and nationalities spread across Central Europe and the upper Balkans. Three-fifths of the Empire's 40 million people were Slavs—Poles, Czechs, Slovaks, Serbs, Bosnians, Montenegrins —but the Empire was ruled by its two non-Slavic races, the Germanic Austrians and the Magyar Hungarians. The structure of government, a dual monarchy, reflected this arrangement: the Emperor of Austria was also the King of Hungary; Austrians and Magyars controlled the bureaucracy; there was place for the Slavs neither at court nor in the government.

Austria-Hungary's nemesis, a nation of free Slavs, the young, independent Kingdom of Serbia, was set close by the sprawling, multinational empire. Serbia's existence acted as a magnet on the restless populations of Austria's South Slav provinces: Bosnia, Herzegovina, and Montenegro. Inside Serbia and in the South Slav provinces, nationalists longed to break up the Hapsburg Empire and weld the dissident provinces into a single Greater South Slav Kingdom. Belgrade, capital of Serbia, was a center of inflammatory Slav propaganda distributed inside the Empire.

Ultimately, either the Emperor Franz Josef or his heir, the Archduke Franz Ferdinand, would decide how Austria would meet the Serbian challenge. If he lived long enough, it would be the Emperor, but in 1914 Franz Josef was eighty-four. His reign of sixty-six years, the longest in modern Europe, had been marked by a sequence of political defeats and personal calamities. The bald little gentleman with muttonchop whiskers had come to the throne in 1848 as a slim, wavy-haired youth of eighteen. He was still a young man when the northern Italian provinces, Lombardy and Venice, were stripped away. Defeat by Prussia in 1866 led to expulsion of Hapsburg influence in Germany. In 1867, Franz Josef's brother, blond, dreamy Maximilian, briefly installed as Emperor of Mexico, was executed by a firing squad on a Mexican hillside. Franz Josef's only son, rakish Crown Prince Rudolf, killed himself and his mistress in a suicide pact at Mayerling. Franz Josef's wife, Empress Elisabeth, once the most beautiful princess in Europe, withdrew after six years of marriage and wandered Europe for four decades until she was struck down by an anarchist's knife. Franz Josef's response to blows was to tighten his emotions and steel himself for further shocks. Facing political challenge, he vowed to maintain the authority of the Crown and the integrity of the Empire. He had no intention of appeasing the South Slavs by modifying the structure of government and giving them a voice.

This conciliatory course was proposed by Franz Josef's nephew and heir. The Archduke Franz Ferdinand, a ponderous, glowering man with brush-cut hair, had offended his uncle by marrying a Bohemian of insufficient rank, Countess Sophie Chotek. The old Emperor insisted that the Archduke renounce the throne for any children he might have from the marriage; Countess Sophie, wife of the Future Emperor, although created a Duchess, was forced in public processions to walk behind the forty-four Hapsburg Archduchesses. Franz Ferdinand himself was restricted to ceremonial functions; he was allowed to inspect army barracks, attend maneuvers, and occasionally to visit provincial capitals. Time was on his side, but he worried that when, eventually, he came to the throne, the disintegration of the Empire would be irreparably advanced. His solution to the problem of nationalist agitation in the South Slav provinces was to reconcile those populations by a radical reconstruction of the structure of the Imperial government: transformation of the Dual Monarchy into a Triad, in which the South Slavs shared power with the Austrians and Magyars. For these views, the Archduke was warmly disliked, especially by the Magyars, who did not relish the thought of diluting their own powerful grip on the Imperial administration.

Meanwhile, another solution for Austria's troubles was growing in popularity: eliminate the source of Slav agitation by crushing Serbia. To the conservative ruling class of the Empire, a preventive war seemed preferable to the kind of decomposition afflicting the Ottoman Empire and more bearable than the protracted negotiations and painful compromises that would be necessary to transform the dual structure into a triad. "Austria," reported the French Ambassador in Vienna on December 13, 1913, "finds herself in an impasse without knowing how she is to escape. . . . People here are becoming accustomed to the idea of a general war as the only possible remedy." The principal advocate of preventive war, General Count Franz Conrad von Hötzendorf, Chief of the General Staff of the Austrian Army, spoke of Serbia as "a dangerous little viper"; he longed to crush the "viper" in its nest. Twice, Austria had mobilized against Serbia, during the Bosnian annexation crisis of 1908–1909 and during the Balkan Wars of 1912–1913. Each time, Conrad had been held back; in 1908, because "at the last moment His Majesty was against it"; in 1912–1913, he complained that he had been "left in the lurch" by Germany.

By 1914, as Conrad knew, the Hapsburg monarchy was too weak to undertake initiatives, military or diplomatic, without assurance of German support. But Conrad also knew that German support must be forthcoming.

Germany Backs Austria-Hungary

The continued existence of Austria-Hungary was vital to the German Empire. Austria was the Reich's only reliable ally. If Austria disintegrated, Germany would face Russia, France, and possibly England alone. In the Wilhelmstrasse, therefore, the preservation of Austria as a Great Power became a cardinal point of German policy. Some German diplomatists worried about this virtually unqualified support for the Hapsburg monarchy. In May

1914, Baron von Tschirschky, the German Ambassador in Vienna, uttered a cry of near despair: "I constantly wonder whether it really pays to bind ourselves so tightly to this phantasm of a state which is cracking in every direction." Tschirschky's cry was ignored. "Our own vital interests demand the preservation of Austria," declared Chancellor von Bethmann-Hollweg.

The Austrian government understood and was prepared to exploit this German predicament. For months, the Kaiser and General von Moltke, Chief of the German General Staff, had given Austria explicit, hearty encouragement to take action against Serbia, even if it meant a German confrontation with Serbia's ally, Russia. On October 26, 1913, the Kaiser had a conversation in Vienna with Count Berchtold, the Austrian Foreign Minister. William began with high-flown talk of the "world historic process," declaring that a war was inevitable in which the Germanic peoples would have to stave off "a mighty impulse of Slavdom." "The Slavs were born to serve and not to rule, and this must be brought home to them," he continued. Specifically, in the case of Serbia, "If His Majesty Francis Joseph demands something, the Serbian Government must yield, and if she does not, then Belgrade will be bombarded and occupied until the will of His Majesty is fulfilled. You may rest assured that I stand behind you and am ready to draw the sword." As he spoke, William moved his hand to the hilt of his sword. The interview concluded with another pledge. "His Majesty ostentatiously used the occasion to assure me that we could absolutely and completely count on him." said Berchtold. "This was the red thread which ran through the utterances of the illustrious Sovereign and when I laid stress on this on taking my departure and thanked him as I left, His Majesty did me the honor to say that whatever came from the Vienna Foreign Office was a command for him."

Moltke had no doubt that war was imminent. He was ready. Like Conrad, he sensed that time was against the Triple Alliance, that the balance of power in Europe was shifting, that Serbia and Russia must be dealt with before the Russian Army was reequipped and the "Slav battering ram" could be driven home. On May 12, 1914, Conrad visited Karlsbad, where Moltke was taking a cure. "General von Moltke expressed the opinion that every delay meant a lessening of our chances," Conrad recorded. The Austrian chief agreed, adding pointedly that "the attitude of Germany in past years has caused us to let many favorable opportunities go by." He asked how long the coming "joint war against Russia and France would last, that is, how long before Germany would be able to turn against Russia with strong forces." Moltke replied, "We hope in six weeks after the beginning of operations to have finished with France, or at least so far as to enable us to direct our principal forces against the East."

Two weeks after the generals met, the Kaiser visited the Archduke Franz Ferdinand at his castle, Konopischt, in Bohemia. The Archduke's garden was famous for its roses and, officially, the German Emperor had come to admire the flowers in bloom. Over two days, William and Franz Ferdinand discussed the dangers posed to the Dual Monarchy and the Triple Alliance by Serbia. They agreed that something must be done. Russia was a factor, but it was the Archduke's opinion that internal difficulties in the Tsar's empire were too great to permit Russia to consider war.

Assassination in Sarajevo

Franz Ferdinand had another appointment at the end of June. He was scheduled to attend array maneuvers in the Bosnian mountains and, as a gesture to the South Slav population, he decided to pay a ceremonial visit to the Bosnian capital, Sarajevo. As a show of goodwill, he asked that the troops normally lining the streets for security during an Imperial visit be dispensed with. Except for a scattering of local policemen, the crowds were to have free access to the Heir to the Throne. On the morning of June 28, Franz Ferdinand, dressed in the pale blue tunic and red-striped black trousers of a cavalry general, with green plumes waving from his cap, sat in the open back seat of the second car, next to his wife, Sophie. Around him on the streets, he saw smiling faces and waving arms. Flags and decorative bright-colored rugs hung from the balconies; his own portrait stared back at him from the windows of shops and houses.

As the procession neared City Hall, the Archduke's chauffeur spotted an object as it was hurled from the crowd. He pressed the accelerator, and a bomb which would have landed in Sophie's lap exploded under the wheels of the car behind. Two officers were wounded and the young bomb-thrower was apprehended by the police. Franz Ferdinand arrived at City Hall shaken and furious. "One comes here for a visit," he shouted, "and is welcomed by bombs." There was an urgent conference. A member of the Archduke's suite asked whether a military guard could be arranged. "Do you think Sarajevo is filled with assassins?" replied the provincial governor.

It was decided to go back through the city by a different route from the one announced. On the way, the driver of the first car, forgetting the alteration, turned into one of the prearranged streets. The Archduke's chauffeur, following behind, was momentarily misled. He started to turn. An official shouted, "That's the wrong way!" At that moment, a slim nineteen-year-old boy stepped forward, aimed a pistol into the car, and fired twice. Sophie sank forward onto her husband's chest. Franz Ferdinand remained sitting upright and for a moment no one noticed that he had been hit. Then the governor, sitting in front, heard him murmur, "Sophie! Sophie! Don't die! Stay alive for our children!" His body sagged and blood from the severed jugular vein in his neck spurted across his uniform. He died almost immediately. Sophie, the Duchess of Hohenberg, died soon after. Fifteen minutes later, both bodies were laid in a room next to the ballroom where waiters were chilling champagne for his reception.

The assassin, Gavrilo Princip, was a native Bosnian, who, on trial, declared that he had acted to "kill an enemy of the South Slavs" and also because the Archduke was "an energetic man who as ruler would have carried through ideas and reforms which stood in our way." Princip was part of a team of youthful assassins, all of whom were Bosnians and thus Austro-Hungarian subjects, belonging to a revolutionary movement whose object was to detach Bosnia and other Slav provinces from the Hapsburg monarchy and incorporate them into a Kingdom of Greater Serbia. They had been provided with six pistols and six bombs taken from the Serbian State Arsenal and smuggled with Serbian help across the frontier. The Serbian government was not involved, but the plot had been hatched in Belgrade. The organizers were members of a secret society of extreme Serbian nationalists known as the Black Hand.

The assassination horrified Europe. Sympathy lay overwhelmingly with the House of Hapsburg. Scarcely anyone questioned Austria-Hungary's right to impose some form of retribution. Sir Edward Grey, looking back, remembered, "No crime has ever aroused deeper or more general horror throughout Europe. . . . Sympathy for Austria was universal. Both governments and public opinion were ready to support her in any measures, however severe, which she might think it necessary to take for the punishment of the murderer and his accomplices." Despite their shock, most Europeans refused to believe that the assassination would lead to war. War, revolution, and assassination were the normal, ingredients of Balkan politics. "Nothing to cause anxiety," announced [the newspaperl *Le Figaro* in Paris. "Terrible shock for the dear old Emperor," King George V noted in his diary.

In Vienna, Franz Josef accepted his nephew's demise with resignation, murmuring, "For me, it is a great worry less." Conrad von Hötzendorf, discreetly ecstatic, hailed the arrival of the long-awaited pretext for preventive war. Now there would be no mere punishment of "the murderer and his accomplices" but the crushing of the "viper," the demolition of the troublesome Serbian state. [Austro-Hungarian foreign minister] Count Berchtold, who hitherto had opposed preventive war, changed his mind and demanded that "the Monarchy with unflinching hand . . . tear asunder the threads which its foes are endeavoring to weave into a net above its head."

12

The Battle of the Marne Produces Stalemate in World War I: September 6–10, 1914

The Allies Stop the German Onslaught

by Winston Churchill

Winston Churchill is known as one of the world's greatest statesmen for his role as leader of England during World War II. In addition to his role as politician, he is remembered for his writing, having been awarded the Nobel Prize for literature in 1953.

In the following selection Churchill writes on the crucial event of World War I—the Battle of the Marne, which occurred in September 1914. The war started a month earlier when Germany attempted to carry out its Schlieffen Plan, in which it launched an all-out attack against France via a German counterclockwise sweep through Belgium with its army's right wing. The plan called for five armies to invade France with one of the armies swinging to the west of Paris in an attempt to trap all French fighting units. During the month of August, the German army of nearly 2 million men, led by Count Helmouth von Moltke, overran Belgium, despite that country's neutrality, and began to enter northern France. Meanwhile, France, under the leadership of General Joseph Joffre, had attempted to enact its own offensive to the east, but it failed due to strong German defensive positions. At the same time, approximately ninety thousand British troops, commanded by Sir John French, had arrived in France and taken part in early battles to slow down the German juggernaut.

Germany's plunge through Belgium and into northern France

Winston Churchill, *The World Crisis*. New York: Charles Scribner's Sons, 1923.

looked unstoppable. However, the most northern of the German armies, the First Army commanded by General Alexander von Kluck and the Second Army under General Karl von Bülow, had temporarily lost contact with the French and British armies. In an attempt to find the enemy, Kluck altered the Schlieffen Plan by heading south instead of continuing a swing to the west of Paris. This change of movement at the beginning of September helped the French and British immensely as the following portion of Churchill's book makes clear. Joffre relied on the help of Ferdinand Foch, who later became supreme Allied commander in the war, to help stem the German tide at the Battle of the Marne described below. This crucial battle, resulting in an end to the German onslaught, brought a stalemate to the front and resulted in the terrible trench warfare that claimed so many lives over the next four years.

As the German armies rolled southwards Paris loomed before them like an enormous breakwater. The enemy capital was not only the heart of France, it was also the largest fortress in the world. It was the center of an intricate spider's web of railways. Masses of troops could debouch in almost unlimited numbers in any direction upon passers-by. No one could count on entering it without a formal siege, the German cannon for which were at this moment deploying before Antwerp. To advance upon both sides of Paris, the Germans had not the troops; to enter Paris, they had not at this moment the guns. What then remained? They must march between Paris and Verdun—which exerted a similar influence—and guarding their flanks from both these fortresses push on to the destruction of the French field armies. Surely also this was the classical tradition? Had not Moltke—not this one but the great Moltke, now dead a quarter of a century—proclaimed 'Direction: Paris! Objective: the enemy's field armies!'

At noon on August 31 a Captain Lepic sent to reconnoitre with his squadron reported from Gournay-sur-Aronde that the interminable columns of Kluck's First Army were turning southeast towards Compiègne instead of continuing their march on Paris. This news was confirmed the next day both by British and French aviators. By nightfall on the 2nd General Maunoury's Sixth Army, which had now arrived in the northern environs of

Paris, reported that there were no German troops west of the line Senlis-Paris. It was upon these indications, confirmed again by British aviators on the 3rd, that [Joseph] Galliéni [commander of French forces defending Paris from the Germans] acted.

Assuredly no human brain had conceived the design, nor had human hand set the pieces on the board. Several separate and discrepant series of events had flowed together. First, the man Galliéni is on the spot. Fixed in his fortress, he could not move towards the battle; so the mighty battle has been made to come to him. Second—the weapon has been placed in his hands—the army of Maunoury. It was given him for one purpose, the defence of Paris; he will use it for another—a decisive manoeuvre in the field. It was given him against the wish of Joffre. It will prove the means of Joffre's salvation. Third, the Opportunity: Kluck, swinging forward in hot pursuit of, as he believed, the routed British and demoralized French, will present his whole right flank and rear as he passes Paris to Galliéni with Maunoury in his hand. Observe, not one of these factors would have counted without the other two. All are interdependent; all are here, and all are here now.

Galliéni realised the position in a flash. 'I dare not believe it,' he exclaimed; 'it is too good to be true.' But it is true. Confirmation arrives hour by hour. He vibrates with enthusiasm. Instantly on the 3rd, he orders the army of Maunoury to positions on the north-east of Paris, which in 48 hours will enable them on the 5th to strike Kluck and with him the whole advancing line of German armies behind their right shoulder blade. But this is not enough. What can one army—hastily improvised—do by itself amid events on such a scale? He must secure the British; he must animate Joffre. At half-past eight on the evening of the 3rd he wrote requesting Joffre's authority for the movement, which he has already ordered Maunoury's army to make, and urging a general offensive by all the French armies between Paris and Verdun simultaneously with his attack.

Joffre and Great Headquarters had arrived that day at Bar-sur-Aube. The numerous bureaux composing the elaborate staff machine had been on the move for two days and were now installing themselves at a new centre. We must not suppose that Joffre and his assistants have not been thinking about things. It was evident to any trained observer that if the fortresses of Verdun and Paris were strongly defended by mobile armies, the German invasion would bulge forward into a wide crescent between these two points; and that this would give an opportunity for a general French attack. Somehow, somewhere, sometime, Joffre and his Staff intended this. In principle they and Galliéni were agreed. From the beginning of the retreat he had said, 'I will attack when my two wings have an enveloping position.' But the How, the Where, and the When. These were the rubs; and on these vital matters it is certain that not only no resolve or design had been formed, but that important orders had been issued inconsistent with such a plan.

Galliéni's messenger reached Bar-sur-Aube on the night of the 3rd, and all the next morning while Maunoury's army was marching into its preparatory stations Galliéni waited in acute anxiety. In the afternoon of the 4th he set off by motor-car to Melun to ask Sir John French for British co-operation. Remember that this man had had Joffre under his command in Madagascar and that he is his formally designated successor. He is not thinking only of the local situation around Paris. He thinks for France and he behaves with the spontaneous confidence of genius in action. But French is out with his troops. Murray, Chief of his staff, receives the Governor of Paris. The interview is lengthy and somewhat bleak.

It was an unpropitious moment for a subordinate French General to propose a new and desperate battle to the British command. On September 2 Sir John French had written to Joffre offering, if the French would turn and fight a general battle on the Marne, to throw in the British Army and put all things to the proof; and Joffre had written back, 'I do not think it possible to contemplate at this moment (*actuellement*) a general operation on the Marne with the whole of our forces.' And the British leader who had braced himself for a supreme ordeal with his small, weary and shot-torn army had been chilled. By a swift reaction, remembering all that had passed since the battle of Mons began, he had reached precipitately but not inexcusably the conclusion that the French had lost heart and did not feel themselves capable of regaining the offensive—at any rate for some time to come. So far, his allies had produced nothing but repulse, defeat and retreat. All their plans, in so far as he was informed of them, seemed to have failed. He knew that the Government was quitting Paris for Bordeaux. He saw that the rearmost lines of places mentioned in Joffre's Instruction No. 2 as the limits of the retreat were far behind the positions he occupied at the moment. He could not exclude from his mind, on the morrow of his offer being declined, the possibility of a general collapse of French resistance. Indeed it was evident that the Germans, by the very fact of disdaining Paris, sought nothing less than the destruction of the French armies. Had he been in the German Headquarters, he would have learned that at this moment Moltke looked confidently forward to driving the French masses either into Switzerland or, if Rupprecht could break through between Nancy and Toul, on to the back of their own eastern fortress line, thus swiftly compelling a universal surrender. . . .

Meanwhile, early on the 4th, Joffre at Bar-sur-Aube had received Galliéni's letter of the night before. All the morning he pondered upon it. Then at noon he authorised Galliéni by telegram to use the army of Maunoury as he had proposed, but with the express condition that it should not attack north, but south of the Marne. A little later he telegraphed to Franchet d' Espérey, now commanding the Fifth French Army, asking him when he could be ready to take part in a general offensive. Franchet replied at 4 p.m. on the 4th that he could attack on the morning of the 6th. This answer reached Joffre between 5 and 6 o'clock. But for the next three hours he did nothing. He took no decision; he sent no orders.

Galliéni arrived back in Paris from Melun shortly before 8 o'clock. He had been absent from his Headquarters for five hours, and meanwhile Joffre's reply to his letter had arrived. He was disturbed by the Commander-in-Chief's express condition that the army of Maunoury should not attack north but only south of the Marne. Other disconcerting news reached him. He heard by telegram from Sir Henry Wilson (Murray's assistant) that the British Army was continuing its retreat; and soon after he received from Colonel Huguet, the French *liaison* officer at the British Headquarters, Sir John French's reply to his proposals: 'Prefer on account of continual changes of the situation to restudy it before deciding on further operations.'

It was now 9 o'clock. Apparently nothing was happening. All the armies would before dawn resume their retreat. So far as he knew, he had received nothing but the permission to make an isolated flank attack with Maunoury's army. Galliéni went to the telephone. He called up Joffre. The Commander-in-Chief came. The two men talked. As the Commander-in-Chief of the French armies circulating his orders through the official channels, Joffre towered above Galliéni; but now, almost in personal contact, Galliéni and his old subordinate spoke at least as equals; and Joffre, to his honour, rising above jealousies and formalities, felt the strong, clear guidance of his valiant comrade. He agreed that Galliéni should attack *north* of the Marne on the 5th, and returning to his circle of officers, ordered the general battle for the 6th. Unfortunately his hesitation and previous delays bred others. We can see from the times quoted how long these vital orders take to prepare and encipher for telegraph, and decipher on arrival. It was nearly midnight before they were dispatched. They were in fact outstripped by duplicates carried by officers in motor cars. Foch, being nearest, received his orders at 1:30 a.m. But neither Franchet nor Sir John French learned of the great decision until after 3 a.m., when their armies had already begun a further day's march to the south.

Nevertheless the die is now cast. The famous order of the day is sent out; and from Verdun to Paris the electrifying right-about-turn points a million bayonets and 1,000 cannon upon the invading hosts. The Battle of the Marne has begun. . . .

We have to remember that the French and British are armies whose springs are compressed back on their reserves and supplies; and that the German armies have hurried on far beyond their rearward organisation and their rail-heads. The French have perfect communications sideways and otherwise; the Germans have not yet restored the broken roads and bridges over which their rapid advance had been made. The French are upon interior lines; the Germans are stretched round the fortified Verdun corner. It was upon this basis that the battle began.

It was less like a battle than any other ever fought. Comparatively few were killed or wounded. No great recognisable feat of arms, no shock proportionate to the event can be discerned. Along a front of more than 200 miles weary, war-ravaged troops were in a loose, desperate contact; then all of a sudden one side sustained the impression that it was the weaker, and that it had had the worst of it. But what was the mechanical causation which induced this overpowering psychological reaction? I can only try to furnish a few links of a chain that is still partly buried.

The popular conception of the Battle of the Marne as a wild counter-rush of France upon Germany, as a leopard spring at the throat of the invaders, as an onslaught carried forward on the wings of passion and ecstasy, is in singular contrast to the truth.

It took some time to turn round the French armies retreating between Verdun and Paris. These ponderous bodies could only effectually reverse their motion after a substantial number of hours and even days. No sooner had the French turned about and begun to advance, than they met the pursuing Germans advancing towards them. Most prudently they stopped at once and fired upon the Germans, and the Germans withered before their fire. It is the Battle of the Frontier fought the other way round. No longer the French advance madly to the strains of the Marseillaise while the German invaders stop and shoot them down with machine guns and artillery; the conditions are reversed. It is the Germans who try to advance and feel for the first time the frightful power of the French artillery. If only the French had done this at the frontiers; if only they had used modern firearms upon hostile flesh and blood at the outset, how different the picture of the world might look to-day!

The Battle of the Marne was won when Joffre had finished his conversation with Galliéni on the night of September 4. Although the French armies had been defeated, had suffered grievous losses, and had retreated day after day, they were still an enormous, unbeaten, fighting force of a very high order. Although the British had retreated with great rapidity and had lost 15,000 men, the soldiers knew they had fought double their numbers and had inflicted far heavier casualties upon the German masses. Drafts and reinforcements had reached them, and they were at the moment of the turn certainly stronger than they had ever been. Although the Germans had 78 divisions on their western front compared to 55 French and British, this superiority was not enough for the supreme objective which they had in view. The Schlieffen plan, the 'receipt for victory,' had prescribed 97 divisions against France alone, and of these 71 were to execute the great offensive wheel through Belgium. Moltke had 19 fewer divisions in the west and 16 fewer in the great offensive wheel. From these again he had withdrawn 2 army corps (4 divisions) to send to the eastern front. He had not thought it worth while to attempt to stop or delay the transport of the British Expeditionary Force across the Channel. According to the German naval history 'the chief of the General Staff personally replied that the Navy should not allow the operations that it would have otherwise carried out to be interfered with on this account. It would even be of advantage if the armies in the west could settle with the 160,000 English at the same time as with the French and Belgians.' Thus when Joffre's decision was taken the balance had already turned strongly in favour of the Allies.

Contrary to the French official narrative, the battle began on the 5th when Maunoury's army came into action on the Ourcq. Let us hasten thither.

General von Kluck's army is marching south and passes Paris in sight of the Eiffel Tower. One of his five corps is acting as flank guard. Bright and cloudless skies! Suddenly about one o'clock the flank corps begins to brush against French troops advancing upon it from Paris. In order to test the strength of their assailants, the Germans attack. At once a violent action flares out and spreads. The French appear in ever-growing strength; the flank guard is beaten. The corps retreats seven miles with heavy losses. The attack from Paris grows and lengthens with more and more weight behind it. Night comes on. The defeated General, hoping to retrieve his fortunes with the morning, sends no word to Kluck. But a German aviator has noticed the conflict far below and the unexpected position of the fighting lines and his report goes to the Army Headquarters. It is not till nearly midnight that Kluck is informed that the shield on which he had counted has been shivered. Then, and not till then did he remember Moltke's orders, namely that in the main advance to drive the French into Switzerland, the armies of Kluck and Bülow should form a defensive flank against attacks from Paris. So far from giving protection to the line of German armies, he has had his own flank torn open; and in four hours another day will break!

So Kluck without more ado pulls back the two corps of his centre, and bids them recross the Marne and form to the north of his defeated flank guard; and as the pressure of Maunoury's attack continues during the 6th, he next takes the last of his army, the two corps of his left, marches them 60 miles in 48 hours, resolved whatever befall not to be out-flanked in the north, and have his communications cut. So here is Kluck who was pressing southward so fast to find the remains of the defeated English, now suddenly turned completely round and drawing up his whole army facing west to ward off Maunoury's continuing attack from Paris. But all this takes time and it is not till the morning of the 9th that Kluck has got himself into his new position and is ready to fall upon Maunoury in superior strength and drive him back upon the Paris fortifications. Meanwhile the war has been going on.

Next in the line to Kluck is Bülow. He too remembers his orders to form a flank guard against Paris. Moreover the withdrawal of Kluck's army corps has left his right in the air. So Bülow pivots on his centre. His right arm goes back, his left arm comes forward, and in the course of the 6th, 7th, 8th and 9th he draws himself up in position facing Paris, and almost at right angles to his previous front. But both Kluck and Bülow have now exposed their left hands to the attack of any allied forces who may he advancing upon them from the south. We know that the British Army and the Fifth French Army (Franchet d'Espérey) have turned about on the morning of the 5th and are advancing. This was only the beginning. Not only had Kluck and Bülow exposed their left flanks to the attack of powerful forces, but a hideous gap had opened between them. A gap of over 30 miles, and practically nothing to fill it with except cavalry! A great mass of cavalry indeed, two cavalry corps, the corps of Marwitz provided by Kluck and of Richthofen provided by Bülow—still only cavalry and without a common commander! An awful gap merely skinned over! We may imagine the feelings of the German Main Headquarters in Luxemburg as this apparition gradually but inexorably resolved itself upon the map. 'If we only had a couple of corps marching forward behind the main front, here is their place and this is their hour.' What did we do with the two corps that were to have besieged Namur?' 'Ah! yes, we sent them to the Vistula! So we did! How far have they got?' 'They are now disembarking from 80 trains 700 miles away.' Well might the Kaiser have exclaimed, 'Moltke, Moltke, give me back my legions!'

If the immense organisms of modern armies standing in a row together find there is a wide gap in their ranks, and have no reserves to come up and fill it, they cannot edge towards one another side-ways like companies or battalions. They can only close the gap by an advance or by a retreat. Which is it to be? To answer this question we must see what has been happening on the rest of the long battle line.

Beginning round the corner at the extreme left of the German invasion, Prince Rupprecht has found he cannot pierce the front between Toul and Epinal. The heavy guns of the French fortresses, the prepared positions and the obstinate armies of Dubail and Castelnau have, with much slaughter, stopped him and his Bavarians. He has been dragging the heavy cannon out of Metz; but it takes a long time to move them. Now they are called for elsewhere. Rupprecht therefore reports on September 8 that he cannot break through the Trouée des Charmes and that he is in fact at a standstill. North-east of Verdun Sarrail faces the army of the German Crown Prince. Here again the guns of the fortress strike heavy blows. The Crown Prince's columns skirting Verdun at a respectful distance are mauled and hampered. Next come the armies of the Duke of Wurtemberg and General von Hausen. These are confronted respectively by the army of de L'Angle le Carré and around the marshes of St. Gond by the army of General Foch.

Throughout the centre the fighting was confused, obscure, and to say the least, indecisive. On the left of Bülow's army (with which was now associated nearly half of Hausen's) an attempt was made to advance against Foch with a desperate, gigantic bayonet attack at dawn. The Germans claim that this assault was successful. The outposts and advance troops of one of Foch's army corps were certainly driven back; but the main line of the French field artillery intact continued its devastating fire. Every one remembers Foch's staccato phrases: 'My flanks are turned; my centre gives way; I attack!'

Three German armies had tried to advance directly against the French and had failed. The French wisely and though hardly with a conscious decision abstaining from their own onslaught, had been content to shoot them down. Broadly speaking, the armies of the German Crown Prince, the Duke of Wurtemburg and General von Hausen were by September 8 at a complete standstill in front of those of Sarrail, de L'Angle and Foch. The centres of the French and German fronts were leaning up against each other in complete equipoise. We are witnessing the birth throes of trench warfare.

But what meanwhile has been happening to the gap? We must not forget the gap. It is still open, thirty miles of it between the two armies of the German right. Into this gap are now marching steadily the British Army together with the left of the Fifth French Army (Franchel's). On they march, these 5 British divisions preceded by 5 brigades of their own cavalry and a French cavalry division. They go on marching. The German aeroplanes see five dark 15-mile long caterpillars eating up the white roads. They report 'heavy British masses advancing.' And what was there to stop them? Only one corps of cavalry now, the other has been called away by Bülow; 6 battalions of Jäger [a German army group], and—a long way back—one rather battered infantry division. There is no possibility of such forces stopping or indeed delaying the march of a professional army of 120,000 men. There are three rivers or streams to cross; four wooded ridges of ground to he cleared. But nothing can prevent this wedge from being driven into the gap. With every hour and every mile of its advance the strategic embarrassments of Bülow and Kluck increased. Nothing had happened so far. The German cavalry and Jäger were being driven back before aggressive British rifle-using cavalry, backed by swiftly gathering bayonets and cannons. But in the whole four days the British lost under 2,000 men. The effects were not tactical; they were strategic.

No human genius planned that the British Army should advance into this gap. A series of tumultuous events had cast them into this position in the line. When they advanced, there was the gap in front of them. On the whole front it was the line of least resistance. Along it they bored and punched, and it led into the strategic vitals of the German right wing. High destiny, blind fate regulated the none too vigorous, but nevertheless decisive, movements of this British Army. It marches on, wondering what has happened to the monster which had pursued it with whip and yell since Mons. Bülow finds his right flank being rolled back by the Fifth French Army, and himself cut off continually from his right-hand comrade, Kluck, by the British advance. Kluck, just as he has got himself into a fine position to fight Maunoury, finds his left and all the rear of his left, hopelessly compromised and exposed.

All these developments present themselves in the first instance upon the maps at Bülow's and Kluck's headquarters, loaded with a hundred details concerning the supplies, the safety and even the escape of at least one-third of the whole of both their armies. And the sum of these disquietudes, unwillingly disclosed item by item, reveals its terrors to the highest centre of authority.

We must now transport ourselves, as is our privilege, to the Emperor's headquarters at Luxemburg. Time: the morning of September 8. The magnates there assembled were already alarmed at the lack of reports of the hourly victories to which they had become accustomed. Instead comes Rupprecht's tale that he is at a standstill. Next there is brought a captured copy of Joffre's battle orders of the 5th. The whole French army is attacking! The Crown Prince says he is pinned down. 'We can make only contemptible advances' he reports. 'We are plagued with artillery fire. The infantry simply get under cover. There are no means of advancing. What are we to do?' The Duke of Wurtemburg and Hausen tell the same tale in similar terms, varied only by the bayonet attack episode. As for Bülow and Kluck, one has only got to look at the map. One does not need to read the tactical reports from these armies, when their strategic torture is disclosed, by aeroplane and other reports. Here at the summit in spacious rooms, in an atmosphere of order, salutes and heel-clicking, far from the cannonade and desperate, squalid, glorious confusion of the fighting lines, the resultants of the pressures upon the immense body of the German invasion of France are totalled and recorded, as if by a Wall Street ticker during a crash of the market. Values are changing from minute to minute. The highest authorities are reconciling themselves to new positions. The booming hopes of the 3rd are replaced by the paper collapse of the 8th. It is the same story in terms of blood instead of scrip.

Colonel Bauer, an accomplished Staff Officer of middle rank, has furnished us with a picture of the scene.

'Desperate panics seized severely the entire army, or to be more correct the greater part of the leaders. It looked at its worst at the supreme command. Moltke completely collapsed. He sat with a pallid face gazing at the map, dead to all feeling, a broken man. General von Stein [Moltke's deputy] certainly said "We must not lose our heads," but he did not take charge. He was himself without confidence and gave expression to his feelings by saying "We cannot tell how things will go." Tappen [head of the Operations Section . . .] was as calm as ever and did not consider that the failure was altogether his fault; nor was it, for he did not lose his nerve. But he did nothing. We younger people could not get a hearing.'. . .

To one of these officers, Colonel Hentsch, the head of the Intelligence, about midday September 8, Moltke imparted his views or mood. Both men are now dead. Neither has left a record of the conversation. We only know what followed from it. Colonel Hentsch got in his long grey car and went along the whole line of the armies, stopping at each of their headquarters and finally reached Bülow's headquarters about dark. He saw his brother Staff Officer of that army. He wrestled with him long. It was agreed between them that if the British Army was actually found to be across the Marne in force and advancing into the gap between Bülow and Kluck, Bülow should retreat to the Aisne in conformity with all the other German armies of the right and centre. Hentsch spared a few moments for a civil chat with old Bülow. The conversation, we are told, was pessimistic. He slept the night at Bülow's headquarters. He started at 7 o'clock the next morning, and the old man not being called till 9, he talked again with the General Staff Officer. It is clear that by this time—the reports of the previous day having been considered—there was no doubt about the heads of the British columns being across the Marne. Therefore the conditions established the night before had been fulfilled. Bülow 'on his own initiative,' as directed by his Staff Officer, ordered the retreat of the Second Army when in due course he entered his Headquarters' office.

Hentsch, knowing what the Second Army was doing, proceeded on his way. He had some difficulty in reaching Kluck. He had to cross the grisly gap and his car was blocked by masses of retreating German cavalry. He was involved in a 'panic,' as he describes it, following a British aeroplane raid. It was not till after noon that he reached Kluck's headquarters. Here again he dealt only with the Staff Officer. He never saw Kluck at all. He told von Kühl, Kluck's Chief of Staff, that as the English were now known to be advancing into the gap, Bülow's army would be retreating. But according to Hentsch, Kühl, some two hours before, had issued an order for retreat. Kühl, who is still alive and has written a massive book, admits that such an order had been telephoned by his subordinate (now dead), but that his subordinate had misconceived what he had intended. He declares that Hentsch gave him a positive order to withdraw Kluck's army to the Aisne, and seeks to lay the whole burden upon him.

At the inquiry into this celebrated episode ordered by Ludendorff in 1917 Colonel Hentsch was exonerated. It was found that his mission from Moltke was in short to see if a retreat was necessary, and if so to co-ordinate the retrograde movements of the five German armies. For this he had been given plenary authority in the name of the Supreme Command. And he had been given it only by word of mouth! But the duel between Kühl and Hentsch has been continued by Kühl over his adversary's grave. He declares the order to retreat was positive. It is however to be noted that he did not ask for this vital order in writing and that he did not tell Kluck about it till several hours had passed.

However it may be, Hentsch, a peripatetic focus of defeat, traversed and retraversed the entire line of the German armies. On the outward journey he gathered evil tidings, and as he returned he issued fateful orders. He used the powers confided to him to order successively the First, Second, Third, Fourth and Fifth German armies to retreat upon the line of the Aisne or in general conformity with that line. Only at one point was any objection raised. The German Crown Prince, who has been so mocked at, received Moltke's emissary in person. Confronted with an order to retreat, he demanded it in writing, and refused otherwise to obey. All Hentsch's directions had been verbal as from one General Staff Officer to another. Here was the first Commander with whom he had come in contact. So he said 'he would have a formal order sent from Luxemburg.' And sent it was by telegraph the next day.

So ended the Battle of the Marne. Until a retreat began, the only Ally army which had crossed the Marne was the British. In fact we may say that along the whole front from Verdun to Paris the French did not advance at all in the Battle of the Marne. Some of them indeed on the left of Foch and the right of Franchet actually retreated. The only Ally army which advanced continually was the British. They advanced northwards in the four days September 5–8 more than 4 miles. But lest the reader should think this an assertion of national vainglory, let me hasten to repeat *first* that at the moment when the British Army was turned round, it had further to go than the others before it came into contact; and *secondly* that when it met the enemy it found in the main only a cavalry screen covering the fatal gap. Nevertheless the fact remains that it probed its way into the German liver.

Thus, by a succession of unforeseeable and uncontrolled events was decided almost at its beginning the fate of the war on land, and little else was left but four years of senseless slaughter. Whether General von Moltke actually said to the Emperor, 'Majesty, we have lost the war,' we do not know. We know anyhow that with a prescience greater in political than in military affairs, he wrote to his wife on the night of the 9th, 'Things have not gone well. The fighting east of Paris has not gone in our favour, *and we shall have to pay for the damage we have done.*'

The Birth of a Nation Becomes the First Blockbuster

by Gerald Mast and Bruce F. Kawin

Movies have become an important art form as well as a huge entertainment industry. Much of the credit for the initial success and acceptance of this relatively new art form goes to D.W. Griffith, a pioneer American producer and director who did his best work between 1908 and 1924.

The following piece is taken from a popular textbook on movies written by Gerald Mast and Bruce F. Kawin. Mast was a film historian as well as a former professor of English and humanities at the University of Chicago. Kawin is professor of English and film studies at the University of Colorado. He is the author of *How Movies Work* and *The Mind of the Novel*. They discuss the source of *The Birth of a Nation*, the controversy surrounding it, and the brilliant techniques Griffith used to create the first blockbuster in film history.

F or his own independent project for 1914, Griffith chose a novel by Thomas Dixon, *The Clansman*. The book appealed to Griffith for several reasons. It was a vast story with a strong hero, covering the final years in the graceful life of the old South before the Civil War; the turbulent, violent years

Gerald Mast and Bruce F. Kawin, *A Short History of the Movies.* New York: Longman, 1971. Copyright © 1971 by Allyn & Bacon, A Pearson Education Company. Reproduced by permission.

of war; and the painful, political years of Reconstruction, during which the Ku Klux Klan arose to defend the rights of the whites. (The prewar and war scenes were Griffith's, not Dixon's.) In addition to this novel, Griffith also used material from the stage version of *The Clansman* and from another Dixon novel, *The Leopard's Spots*, all of which were extremely racist. Griffith, a Southerner whose father served in the Confederate Army, was attracted by Dixon's slant. Dixon, also a Southerner, saw the Reconstruction era as a period of chaos in which the "civilized" white South, presented as the gallant underdog, struggled but survived. It was this film, with its inflammatory messages and dangerous social and political implications, that Griffith set out to make. Shooting began on the Fourth of July, 1914.

The project was vast: It took six weeks to rehearse and nine weeks to shoot, an incredible amount of time in an era when most films were cranked out in a week. It required thousands of people and animals and many huge and detailed indoor sets. Its cost, $110,000, was the most ever invested in a motion picture. At the film's official premiere in Clune's Auditorium in Los Angeles on February 8, 1915, audiences finally saw how huge Griffith's plan and project were. The 13-reel film was still called *The Clansman* at that opening. When the author of the novel finally saw the film, however, Dixon told Griffith, in his enthusiasm, that the original title was too tame. Griffith should call his film *The Birth of a Nation.* Dixon's point was that the nation was truly born only when the whites of the North and South united "in defense of their Aryan birthright." For Griffith, the "real nation" began when North and South united to heal the wounds of the Civil War and Reconstruction; in a 1915 interview he said that "there can exist no union without sympathy and oneness of sentiments." While he did not acknowledge the racism that was part of that shared sentiment, he credited the KKK with beginning "the birth." Dixon's and Griffith's interpretations of the title were not all that different.

The retitled version opened in New York on March 3, 1915, still 13 reels long. But in response to social protests, Griffith deleted about nine minutes from the film (footage that has never been recovered), leaving it just over 12 reels long. The most complete surviving version lasts three hours.

The Birth of a Nation is as much a document of American social history as of film history. Though President Wilson, a former historian at Princeton, described the film as "like history written with lightning," its action openly praises the Ku Klux Klan. Wilson may well have offered the simile to help his old school chum, Dixon. The film, which contributed significantly to the resurgence of the Klan in the 20th century, is a very difficult morsel for today's liberal or social activist to swallow. It was just as difficult for the liberals of 1915. The NAACP, the president of Harvard, social activist Jane Addams, and liberal politicians all damned the work for its bigoted, racist portrayal of the Negro. The film was suppressed in some cities for fear of race riots; politicians spoke for or against it according to their dependence on the black vote. At a revival of the film some ten years after its original opening, mobs poured into Chicago to see it as well as to attend a Ku Klux Klan convention. With all of the controversy over the film, it might be wise to look at Griffith's handling of the black man and woman before moving on to other aspects of the picture.

Two of the three villains—Lynch (the false reformer) and Sarah (Stoneman's mistress)—are not pure Negroes but mulattoes. Both possess qualities that Griffith had already damned in whites—hypocrisy, selfishness, social reforming, and sexual license. That they were mulattoes may indicate that Griffith's main target was not the blacks but miscegenation—an objective of the third villain, a black soldier named Gus, when he forces his attentions on a Southern white girl. (His marriage proposal—a rape in the novel—causes Flora, the "little pet sister," to throw herself off a cliff to her death; in the novel, and reportedly in the censored footage, Gus is castrated by the KKK when they kill him.) The miscegenation theme flows through the movie like a poisonous river—in the scenes of the lecherous black legislature, in signs at the black-dominated polling place, in Lynch's attraction to Elsie (Lillian Gish) and Gus's to Flora (Mae Marsh), and in the outrages that drive the hero, Ben Cameron (Henry B. Walthall), to dream up the KKK. The mixing of bloods is one of the principal sources of "evil" in this picture. Griffith's stance against miscegenation stems from an assumption about blacks and whites that is perhaps more central to the film's offensiveness. For Griffith, whites are whites and blacks blacks; the white race is naturally superior; each race has "its own place." If Griffith's view seems outrageous—well, it is. Not every masterpiece is "politically correct," and part of dealing with *The Birth of a Nation* lies in examining, rather than explaining away, how offensive it is. Although Griffith recognized that slavery was the root of America's racial problems, his solution (proposed in part of the censored footage, an ending originally meant to balance the all-white harmony of the surviving conclusion) was to send the blacks back to Africa.

There are "good" blacks and "bad" blacks in Griffith's film. The good ones are the "faithful souls" who "know their place" and stay with their white family after the war. *Gone With the Wind*, 24 years newer fashioned than *The Birth of a Nation* and still adored by the public, makes the same distinction between good and bad "darkies." Perhaps Griffith's most offensive scene is the one in which the empty state legislature suddenly (with the aid of a dissolve) springs to life, full of black lawmakers with bare feet on desks, swilling booze and eating fried chicken while they eye the white women in the gallery. But Griffith's treatment of these blacks is not an isolated expression of racial prejudice; it is a part of his lifelong distrust of the "evils" of social change and disruption. (To be consistent, of course, he should also have denounced the KKK as a disruptive social movement—but he evidently saw its actions as restorative.)

The Power of the Movie

The key to *The Birth of a Nation* is that it is both strikingly complex and tightly whole. It is a film of brilliant parts carefully tied together by the driving line of the film's narrative. Its hugeness of conception, its acting, its sets, its cinematic devices had not been equaled by any film before it and would not be surpassed by many that followed it. Yet surprisingly, for such an obviously big picture, it is also a highly personal and intimate one. Its small moments are as impressive as its big ones. Though Griffith summarizes an entire historical era in the evolution of the nation in general and the South in particular, his summary adopts an intimate, personal focus: two families, one from the North (the Stonemans), one from the South (the Camerons), who, despite the years of death and suffering, survive the Civil War and Reconstruction. The eventual marriage between the two white families becomes a symbol or emblem for Griffith's view of the united nation. Love, courage, sincerity, and natural affection triumph over progressive movements and selfish reformers. The close observation of people and their most intimate feelings, the techniques of which Griffith had been developing for five years, propels the film, not its huge battle scenes, its huge dances and political meetings, or its detailed "historical facsimiles" of Ford's Theater and the Appomattox courthouse. The big scenes serve as the violent social realities with which the central characters must contend.

Even in the mammoth battle sequences Griffith never deserts his human focus. His rhythmic and energetic editing constantly alternates between distant, extreme long shots of the battles and close concentration on the individual men who are fighting. Griffith takes the time for such touches as his cut from the living, fighting soldiers to a shot of the motionless dead ones who have found "War's peace," or his cuts from the valiant effort on the Union side to shots of a similar effort on the Confederate, including Ben Cameron's heroic charge of the Union lines, ramming the Southern flag down the barrel of a Union cannon. Griffith increases the power, the violence, the energy of these battle sequences with his sensitivity to cutting on contrary movement across the frame, to cutting in rhythm with the action, and to cutting to different distances and angles that mirror the points of view of the different participants. But in the midst of such violence, Griffith takes time for quiet moments: the moment when the two boys, one Cameron and one Stoneman, die in each other's arms; the moment in which a mother on a hilltop views the invading army in the valley.

This shot, one of the most celebrated in the film, shows Griffith's control of the masking or irising effect, another of the techniques he and [chief photographer Billy] Bitzer had explored at [the motion picture company] Biograph. The *iris shot* masks a certain percentage of the frame, concentrating the viewer's attention completely on a circle of light within the blackened screen rectangle. . . . (The iris is a circular mask; other masks could create an image in the shape of a keyhole or show just half the screen—essential for the early matte shots, which were made in the camera—or be cut into any shape of light.) The iris, analogous to the theatre spotlight or today's zoom lens, either shrinks the audience's attention from the whole field to a single point or expands it from the single point to the whole field. G.A. Smith used an unmoving iris to frame his point-of-view close-ups in *Grandma's Reading Glass* and *As Seen Through the Telescope* (both 1900). In *The Birth of a Nation*'s most famous iris shot, Griffith begins tightly on the weeping mother's face and then irises out to reveal the awesome army below her, the cause of her sorrow. Of the many masking shots that reveal cause and effect, or event and context, in the picture, this is the one that most brilliantly uses the iris to work with near and far views in a single but redefined visual field.

Griffith often uses animals as symbols or to define his characters and their emotional states. In the early sequence depicting the gentle, peaceful life of the old South (analogous to the opening sequence of *Judith of Bethulia*), Doctor Cameron strokes two puppies. Significantly, one of the puppies is black and the other white; it is also significant that a kitten soon begins to play with the pups and starts a fight. The dogs become visual metaphors for Griffith's idealized prewar South, a happy mixture of different races and social classes, able to work out their own problems; the cat is the intrusive (Northern) outsider who hurts the white pup. Later in the film Griffith cross-cuts between the two lovers, Elsie and Ben, gently playing with a dove, and the savage Lynch as he mistreats a dog. As in most of his films, the characters' attitudes toward animals reveal their attitudes toward people.

Another of Griffith's artistic devices is his use of the main street in the town of Piedmont as a barometer of the film's emotional and social tensions. At the film's opening the street is full of people and carriages: active, sociable, friendly. As the Confederate soldiers first march off to war, the street becomes a carnival: fireworks, cheering townspeople, rhythmic columns of men on horses. When "the little Colonel" (Ben Cameron) returns home after the war, the street is desolate, ruined, dusty. And finally, when the town is overrun with carpetbaggers and reconstructionists, drunken gangs of blacks rove the street; the street has become a very unfriendly, ungentle place. By capturing emotion in concrete images Griffith successfully renders feeling— rather than a parody of feeling, as in *Queen Elizabeth.*

Griffith never deserts the principles of his early melodramatic one-reelers as the means to keep his story moving. The suspense and excitement of Griffith's cross-cutting create the dramatic tension of many of the sequences: the attack of a band of black renegades (significantly their captain is white) on the defenseless town and the Cameron home; the assassination of Lincoln in Ford's Theater; the rapacious Gus chasing the youngest Cameron sister through the woods until she jumps to her death. The most thrilling and upsetting sequence of all is the climax, in which Griffith gives us not one but two last-minute rescues. Griffith

cross-cuts between two sets of victims and their common res-
cuers—the Ku Klux Klan—furiously galloping forth to eradicate
the forces of rapine and death and social change. Not only is this
rescue sequence Griffith's most complex up to this point, it is
also his most sensitive to the kinetic excitement of editing
rhythms and the moving camera.

But after the dust from the galloping climax has settled, Griffith makes fun of the blacks who retreat from the ballot box in
fear of the Klan—and then, moving from the infuriating to the
ridiculous, he celebrates the peaceful union of Elsie Stoneman
and Ben Cameron with a superimposed allegorical pageant in the
heavens. Elsie and Ben see Christ replacing the military general;
Christ cuts the Gordian knot, and all humanity rejoices as the
City of God replaces the Kingdoms of the Earth. There are several remarkable things about this closing vision: its audacity, its
irrelevance, and the passion and sincerity of Griffith's commit-
ment to it. But exactly how is this City of God to become a reality? Certainly not by the efforts of the Ku Klux Klan alone. It is
the evil in the human soul that must be exorcised. And once
again Griffith reveals his nearsightedness in probing what he
considers evil.

Griffith's View of Evil

The evil in the film is instigated by three people. They are evil
(1) because they are evil or (2) because they have mixed blood.
They succeed in doing evil because they entice the easily
tempted Congressman Stoneman to the abolitionist cause. In the
misguided Stoneman, Griffith takes another potshot at social reformers. Stoneman's temptation stems from his vanity despite
his physical deformity (Griffith uses a club foot, parallel to the
classic deformity of Shakespeare's Richard III, and an ill-fitting
wig to define these traits) and from the "fatal weakness" of being sexually attracted to his mulatto housekeeper. According to
the film's action, the chaos of the Civil War was the direct result
of the nation's Stonemans, who became entangled in an evil of
which they were totally ignorant or that they unwisely thought
they could control. Even granting Griffith this preposterous
premise, how is one to be sure the future contains no Stonemans?
And how can one abolish slavery without abolition? *The Birth
of a Nation*'s final vision is an innocent and mystical wish rather
than the intellectual consequence of what preceded it. The film

remains solid and engaging as a big, complex narrative and a formal cinematic achievement, flimsy and repulsive as social theory . . . a powerful story of love, loss, and endurance. [Movie executive Harry] Aitken and Griffith, who had set up their own company (Epoch) to finance and distribute *The Birth of a Nation*, had by now left Mutual for the Triangle Film Corporation, whose big three were Griffith, Thomas Ince, and Mack Sennett. But the controversy over *The Birth* led to Griffith's pulling *The Mother and the Law* from Triangle's release schedule; instead he and Aitken set up another separate company (Wark) to produce *Intolerance* (1916).

Griffith's treatment of blacks provoked public condemnation, even riots. The criticism stung Griffith deeply, since he felt he had gone to some trouble to present good and bad blacks *and* whites, as he had watered down or cut out the novel's most inflammatory, racist passages. . . . Unfortunately, *The Birth of a Nation* used the medium so powerfully that Griffith's film unexpectedly but indisputably inspired the birth of the 20th-century Klan in late 1915.

Griffith began defending himself against the charges of bigotry and hatred; he angrily protested the film's suppression in several cities and wrote *The Rise and Fall of Free Speech in America*, a pamphlet that championed the "Freedom of the Screen." *Intolerance* was to be his cinematic defense, his pamphlet in film form against intellectual censorship. Fortunately for Griffith, *The Birth of a Nation* became the first authentic blockbuster in film history, earning untold millions of dollars.

EVENT 14

America's Entry Signals the Defeat of Germany: April 6, 1917

Woodrow Wilson Leads the United States into War

by Harvey A. DeWeerd

Harvey A. DeWeerd was a teacher and writer. He authored *Great Soldiers of Two Wars* and was a contributing editor for *Army Infantry Journal*. In this selection DeWeerd explains how the United States became involved in World War I: German aggression in 1914, various German plots to undermine American war preparation, and Germany's unrestricted submarine warfare. Of these, DeWeerd focuses on one German plot, the Zimmerman note. This note was a message from Germany to Mexico that was intercepted by the British, who showed it to American officials. This note indicated Germany had approached Mexico in hopes of creating an alliance between the two countries in case of war with the United States. To compensate the Mexican government for its proposed alliance, Germany promised to help it regain portions of land lost to the United States after the Mexican War. In addition, DeWeerd claims Germany's unrestricted submarine warfare pushed America into the European conflict. DeWeerd notes that America's men, machines, and morale were crucial to bringing an end to the war.

The United States accomplishments in World War I can only be partly quantified. The great share of its contribution toward winning the war was in the intangible sphere of lead-

Harvey A. DeWeerd, *President Wilson Fights His War: World War I and the American Intervention*. New York: Macmillan Company, 1968. Copyright © 1968 by Harvey A. DeWeerd. Reproduced by permission.

ership, influence, and morale. Yet the statistics are impressive. Starting from a base of almost complete unpreparedness for war, the United States brought 4,800,000 men into the armed services between April 6, 1917, and November 11, 1918. This was twice the number of men involved in the armed services of the North during the Civil War. Most of these four million men received some training, on the average six months in the United States, and those who went overseas averaged two months additional training in France.

Within a year and a half of the outbreak of war, the United States transported two million men to France, the greater share of them in British ships. Twenty-nine large American divisions, the equivalent of at least fifty-eight European divisions, more than a million men, were engaged in combat before the armistice. These troops faced one fourth of the German divisions on the western front from September 12 to November 11, 1918, and defeated them in battle, driving them from one of the strongest positions in France and cutting the important German lateral communication lines at Sedan. . . .

Before it was in a position to achieve these results, the United States helped to defeat the German U-boat menace by participating in the convoy system, by creating the North Sea mine barrage, and by building merchant ships on a large scale. In France a vast program of port construction, base building, communications installation, and augmenting of railways was completed. This extensive logistics construction could not be built up gradually over four years as the Allied systems were developed, but had to be created in less than two years.

The official American military program called for the presence in France by July 1, 1919, of eighty divisions of troops. With corps and army troops this would have amounted to about four million men. This massive troop program, by its mere existence, greatly encouraged the French and British during the dark hours of the German offensives in 1918. To the same extent it discouraged the Germans and their allies. Whether or not the United States could have carried out the eighty-division program if the war had continued remains a question, but post-armistice military construction in the United States was on such a scale as to suggest that it might have been done. Had this been the case, the United States would have had as many troops in France as Britain and France put together. With forces of this magnitude in the field,

Firing a thirty-seven-millimeter gun, American soldiers
attack a German-held position in France in 1918.

American control over military operations would have increased.

A campaign in 1919, had one occurred, would have been influenced by the ideas of Brigadier General William Mitchell for the use of tactical aircraft and parachute drops; it would have been accompanied by a strategic bombing program being worked out by General Hugh Trenchard, and would have seen the massed employment of tanks and armored personnel carriers as advocated by John F.C. Fuller.

This, however, is in the field of speculation. Less speculative was the fact that the American military program enabled the British and the French to recover from their defeats of 1918 more rapidly than otherwise would have been the case. The appearance in France of two million American troops permitted the Allies greater freedom of action earlier than otherwise would have been the case. They used their forces offensively in 1918 to a far greater extent than would have been prudent if the American Army had not been coming into France as a growing reserve.

One element of the American contribution was the imparting of a spirit of the offensive to the tired Allied forces with whom they served. The American troops set a standard of offensive spirit in the attack, which the Allied forces found it hard to ignore. The service of the United States First and Second Divisions with the French Tenth Army in July 1918 comes to mind, as well as that of the Third, Fourth, Twenty-eighth, Thirty-second, Forty-second, and Seventy-seventh Divisions in the French Sixth Army in the reduction of the Marne salient. The surge of fresh American forces into France counteracted the spirit of defeatism that developed in that country after the defeat of the Nivelle offensive in 1917. No one could look at the apparently endless columns of khaki-clad American soldiers coming into France and entertain the idea of defeat. As one English observer said: "The coming of the United States Army lightened weary hearts."

On the German forces in France there was an equal but contrary effect. They saw physical evidence that the German submarine campaign had failed. Two million American soldiers in France changed the German military situation radically. For the first time in the war, German soldiers entertained the idea of being defeated, something they felt could not have been done by Britain and France alone. This impression of the size of the American military effort was coupled with a recognition of the position of leadership in the Western world occupied by President Wilson. Speaking for a vast and youthful country whose manpower and resources seemed to be inexhaustible, making no claims for territorial or financial awards, President Wilson, through a series of memorable addresses, made it possible for the Germans to think of ending the war on terms less than victory. It was easier for the Germans to accept a disarming armistice at the hands of Wilson than those of Lloyd George or Clemenceau.

Writing in the postwar years to the German Reichstag on the origin, execution, and collapse of the German offensives of 1918, General Kuhl summed up the effect of the American intervention as follows:

> The American soldier showed himself full of courage, even if he lacked experience. Fresh, well-fed, and with strong nerves that had known no strain, he advanced against the German Army, which was exhausted by the unprecedented efforts of four years of war. In this and in the great numerical reenforcements which the Americans brought to our opponents at the decisive moment lies the importance of America's intervention.

15 The Balfour Declaration:
November 2, 1917

The British Call for a Jewish Homeland

by Will Varner

Dr. Will Varner, head of The Master's College Israel/Bible Extension Campus, has written *Jacob's Dozen* and other works dealing with Israel's history.

In the following piece, Varner talks of the reasons and the people behind the Balfour Declaration.

Palestine had been the ancient Jewish homeland for hundreds of years after ancient Israelite tribes conquered the land under Joshua and later leaders of the Old Testament period. Armies from various nations had eventually displaced and scattered the Jews following the time of Jesus.

Severe persecutions caused many Jews to emigrate from Europe back to Palestine in the 1800s. In 1882 groups of Jewish youths formed a movement to promote further immigration to Palestine. Zionism was born, a movement dedicated to establishing a national homeland for Jews in Palestine. Theodor Herzl, a reporter, organized the Zionist movement worldwide by setting up the First Zionist Congress in Basel, Switzerland, in 1897. At first, the Zionists attempted to get Turkey to grant a charter for a settlement in Palestine, but they had no luck. In 1903 Great Britain offered the Zionists the Uganda Plan, in which the English would give up part of British East Africa for a Jewish settlement, but the Zionists rejected the plan since they had their hearts set on the ancient land of Israel for a home.

Will Varner, "Behind the Balfour Declaration," www.foigm.org, June 12, 2003. Copyright © 2003 by Will Varner. Reproduced by permission.

When World War I broke out, several things happened that led to the creation of the Balfour Declaration. England, France, and Russia, known as the Allies, fought against Germany, Austria-Hungary, and Turkey, which held Palestine. England wished to wrest Palestine as well as other holdings in the Middle East from Turkey to protect its valuable Suez Canal. At the time, Arabs of the Middle East were subjected to Turkish control; the British wished to use these discontented people against their Turkish masters. England agreed to recognize and support Arab independence if the Arab people would join the British war effort. In early 1916 England, France, and Russia conducted a series of negotiations that resulted in the Sykes-Picot Agreement, which allocated postwar spheres of influence for the Allies in the Arab world.

The most prominent events marking the early days of the modern Zionist movement were the publication of Theodor Herzl's *The Jewish State* in 1896 and his calling of the First Zionist Congress in 1897. Herzl recognized that if the Zionist dream of a homeland for the Jewish people was to be realized, international approval of the idea had to be secured. He spent the remainder of his short life seeking such approval, but he died in 1904, disappointed at his failure to do so. The Great War, now known as World War I, further threatened those dreams. Turkey, Germany's main ally, had been in control of the Holy Land for nearly 400 years. If international approval for a Jewish homeland was to be secured, it would have to be sought through an Allied victory in the war. The best hope for such an approval lay with Great Britain, whose far-flung empire demonstrated that it was already engaged in the *great game* of international colonialism.

Before the end of the war, at a time when British hopes were buoyed by their invasion of the Middle East under General Edmund Allenby, the British cabinet issued the famous Balfour Declaration. Arthur James Balfour, Foreign Secretary in the British government, communicated the following memo to Lord Rothschild, head of the Zionist Federation in Great Britain, on November 2, 1917:

I have the pleasure in conveying to you, on behalf of His Majesty's Government, the following declaration of sympathy with the Jewish Zionist aspirations which have been submitted to, and approved by, the Cabinet.

"His Majesty's Government views with favour the establishment in Palestine of a national home for the Jewish people, and will use our best endeavors to facilitate the achievement of this object, it being clearly understood that nothing shall be done which may prejudice the civil and religious rights of existing non-Jewish communities in Palestine, or the rights and political status enjoyed by Jews in any other country."

Finally, after nearly 40 years of building Jewish settlements in the Holy Land and 20 years after the Zionist Congress, international recognition by a major world power for a Jewish homeland had been secured. Much has been written about the political and strategic issues behind the Balfour Declaration. Many reasons have been given for its issuance. The full story, however, may not be given in the standard history books.

What events and circumstances caused the British government to publicly back the Zionist dream of a homeland for the dispersed Hebrews?

The Reasons

In most of the historical accounts of this period, at least three reasons are given for the British decision. While all three played a definite role in shaping British attitudes, a fourth probably was the most decisive.

What are the reasons for the Balfour Declaration?

1. The British government had a great desire to maintain an open channel through the Middle East to its extensive possessions in India and East Africa. A Jewish homeland, under British sponsorship, could maintain that freedom of access, which had been cut off by the Ottoman Turkish holdings in the region. Jewish control of Palestine, therefore, was in England's best interest.

2. The British government wanted to keep the Russians in the war and persuade the Americans to enter the war. A decision to favor the Zionist cause would encourage both Russian and American Jews to influence their governments to join with Britain and the Allies in the fight against the Germans and Turks. While this probably overestimated the political power of the Russian and American Jews, it is one of the reasons most often cited.

3. The British government wanted to reward the brilliant

chemist and Zionist leader, Chaim Weizmann, for his help in the war effort when he developed a process to synthesize acetone, an ingredient necessary for producing the explosives that were in extremely short supply. While Weizmann certainly did help the British war effort, this tale, later told by Lloyd George, was largely invented. Weizmann never mentioned it in his autobiography, *Trial and Error.*

Historians debate and wrangle over the degree to which these three factors influenced the British cabinet to issue the Balfour Declaration. However, none of the three, nor all of them together, seem to be sufficient reasons for the positive British view. When we consider the Christian beliefs of the major members of the cabinet, we can conclude that the biblical teaching of Israel's return to Zion was the main reason that the cabinet was moved to issue the Balfour Declaration.

The Men

Who were the main players in this decision, and what did they believe about Israel in Bible prophecy?

David Lloyd George was the Prime Minister. Unlike many other British lawmakers, Lloyd George was not educated in schools that stressed the Greek and Latin classics, but was brought up on the Bible. He often remarked that the names of biblical places were better known to him than were those of the battles that figured in the war. He was reared in the centuries-old movement in British evangelical thought that stated that the British should take the lead in restoring the Jews to Zion. He was but the latest in a long line of Christian Zionists in Britain that stretched back to the Puritans. Guided by the Scriptures, this "restoration" movement, as it was called, believed that the advent of the Messiah would occur once the Jewish people were restored to their native land. Lloyd George wanted his country to carry out what he regarded as the Lord's work in the Middle East. His own words about the Balfour Declaration are clear:

> It was undoubtedly inspired by natural sympathy, admiration and also by the fact that, as you must remember, we had been trained even more in Hebrew history than in the history of our own country. I could tell you all the kings of Israel. But I doubt whether I could have named half a dozen of the kings of England!

Another member of the cabinet, Jan Christian Smuts from

South Africa, earlier had fought the British in the Boer War. Steeped in the Bible, Smuts strongly supported the Zionist ideas. He later wrote in his personal memoirs, "The people of South Africa have been brought up almost entirely on Jewish tradition. The Old Testament has been the very marrow of Dutch culture here in South Africa." He had been brought up to believe that "the day will come when the words of the prophets will become true, and Israel will return to its own land."

Arthur James Balfour, influenced by the Scot Presbyterian branch of his family, was also raised on the Bible. His support of Zionism, however, was also based on his sympathy for an oppressed people who had suffered in exile for far too long. Balfour believed that the Jewish genius could be channeled into a productive nation in their original land. When asked why the Jew should be privileged with such an honor, he replied, "The answer is that the position of the Jew is unique. For them race, religion and country are inter-related as they are inter-related in the case of no other religion and no other country on earth."

Lloyd George, Smuts, and Balfour comprise but a sampling of the many Christian Zionists in British circles who were motivated by biblical concerns. While the political, military, and strategic reasons that led the British cabinet to issue the Balfour Declaration cannot be discounted, it is this last influence that needs to be noticed and stressed. Without this biblical predisposition, the Balfour Declaration would not have been issued. A secular historian concludes, "Biblical prophecy was the first and most enduring of the many motives that led Britons to want to restore the Jews to Zion" (David Fromkin, *A Peace to End All Peace*, p. 298).

16

The Russian Revolution: Communists Take Over the Government: November 7–15, 1917

Lenin and the Bolsheviks Take Over Russia

by Alan Moorehead

Alan Moorehead has written extensively on historical subjects in such books as *Gallipoli, Eclipse, The White Nile, The Blue Nile, Montgomery, Darwin and the Beagle,* and *The March to Tunis.* In the following selection Moorehead describes the tumultuous events that occurred over a ten-day period in 1917 that brought Lenin to power in Russia, forever changing not only that nation but many others.

In order to understand the story that he tells, we need to consider the crucial times that led up to it. Russia had been ruled by czars, who ran things with an iron grip. By the late 1800s the peasants and industrial workers, who were extremely poor and lived with terrible working conditions, grew discontented. Various political parties formed in an attempt to remedy the situation, including some pro-Western ones as well as Marxists. In 1898 the Marxists set up the Russian Social Democratic Labor Party, which split a few years later into two groups—the Bolsheviks, the majority, and the Mensheviks, the minority. The leader of the Bolsheviks was Vladimir Ulyanov, who went by the name of Lenin.

Due to economic problems and a failed war with Japan in 1904, discontent grew among the people of Russia. In 1905 unarmed workers who had marched to the czar's Winter Palace in St. Petersburg, later renamed Petrograd, were gunned down by government

---

Alan Moorehead, *The Russian Revolution.* New York: Harper & Row, 1958. Copyright © 1958, renewed 1986 by Time, Inc. Reproduced by permission.

troops. Revolutionaries in the city established a council, called a
soviet, to act as a voice for their concerns. Other soviets were soon
set up in several Russian cities. Despite the discontent, the czar,
Nicholas II, gave up very little power to a newly constituted parliament, the Duma.

World War I, a disaster for Russia, led to the end of the czar's
rule. In 1914 and 1915 German forces crushed Russian troops re-
peatedly, and the war created tremendous hardships for the civilians
at home. In March 1917 riots broke out in Petrograd, and government troops joined the side of the protestors. Because he had lost all
support, Nicholas abdicated. The Duma tried to run the country, but
revolutionaries continued to press for more radical changes. Armed
workers and soldiers in July of the same year tried but failed to
overthrow the government in Petrograd, with the result that Lenin
had to flee the country and his followers scattered. In the same
month the socialist Alexander Kerensky became premier and continued the war effort. In late October Lenin secretly made his way
back to Russia where he met his coconspirators in Petrograd. He
urged an immediate rebellion, but others were concerned about
whether the Bolsheviks could carry their rebellion to Moscow and
beyond. Lenin depended heavily on his second-in-command, the
gifted writer and orator Leon Trotsky. After deciding to go ahead
with the rebellion, the Bolsheviks and their opponents, led by
Kerensky, conducted a confused struggle to win the hearts of the
soldiers over the next few days.

Moorehead begins the following selection on November 5 when
both sides realized the maneuvering was over and the actual fight
was beginning. The Bolsheviks gradually took over one stronghold
after another in Petrograd until Kerensky in desperation left to find
loyal troops outside the city. Only the Winter Palace was still in
government hands. Bolsheviks attacked it, causing many people in
the city who opposed the Bolsheviks to set up a Committee for the
Salvation of the Country and Revolution. Moorehead continues the
dramatic story by showing how the struggle intensified between the
two sides as troops and civilians were trying to decide between support for the Bolsheviks or the Committee for Salvation. Kerensky
could find no troops willing to fight for him, resulting in the final
collapse of the government. Petrograd was secured by the Bolsheviks, and Moscow soon followed. By November 15, only ten days
after the coup began, Lenin's triumph was complete.

On Monday, November 5, negotiations with Polkovnikov [a pro-Kerensky military leader] were resumed, and the Bolsheviks now demanded that they be given a place in the staff conferences of the Petrograd Military District. When this was refused telegrams were sent out from Smolny to the regiments ordering them to occupy strategic points in their areas with machine guns.

Now at last the government began to take serious action. Kerensky called a cabinet meeting late in the evening of November 5, and an emergency was declared. Polkovnikov was put in command of all forces in the city, with orders to take drastic action against disturbances. The Soviet Military Revolutionary Committee was declared illegal, and an order was sent out for the arrest of Trotsky and other Bolshevik leaders. Bolshevik newspapers were banned. Kerensky continued to be confident; he said he knew all about the Bolshevik plans. He would be glad if they did attempt a rising; he had ample forces to deal with it. Even now loyal troops were being summoned from outside the city. Yet Polkovnikov took no drastic action on this night. He sent off a Women's Battalion* to strengthen the guard inside the Winter Palace, but he made no attempt at all to attack the real center of the trouble, Smolny. And in fact the government had already suffered a major reverse on this day without a single shot being fired.

The garrison of the Fortress of St. Peter and St. Paul was made up of gunners and a bicycle battalion, and they had been none too friendly to the Bolsheviks. They had rejected the Bolshevik commissar who had been sent to them, and it was clear that if they did not actually oppose a rising they would remain neutral. As a last resource Trotsky was asked to address the men. Trotsky in his own account passes over this incident with a fair show of modesty, but it seems clear that he must have risen to heights of oratory, for he won the garrison over, and that meant control of the arsenal as well. During the night about ten thousand small arms were handed out to the Red Guards, who were now organized in battalions of five to six hundred men in all the larger factories.

The last hours of political maneuvering were running out very quickly. Early in the morning of November 6 Polkovnikov cut the telephone lines to Smolny, and detachments of loyal troops

* This was a volunteer force of patriotic women who had sworn to fight to the death against the Germans.

attempted to occupy the printing shops of the Bolshevik news-papers. The cruiser *Aurora*, always a doubtful center of loyalty, was ordered to leave the Neva for the open sea. Officer cadets from Oranienbaum and other troops which were reputed to be reliable were instructed to march into the city. The Bolsheviks, however, were not so easily cut off. Red Guards stood sentry over the printing shops, and the Bolshevik papers came out at noon with inflammatory appeals for action. In Smolny Trotsky and his Military Revolutionary Committee still had the use of other means of communication, and a stream of defiant orders was sent out to the military garrison: the *Aurora* was not to move, the reg-iments which had been ordered by the government into the city were to stay where they were, and the Petrograd garrison itself was to stand ready for action. A further call went out to Kron-stadt urging the sailors to come to the capital without delay. . . .

The American correspondent John Reed has left us a remark-able description of Petrograd through these critical days. In his *Ten Days That Shook the World* he makes us feel as no one else has done what it was like to be there, especially if you happened to be a foreigner and an avid supporter of the Bolsheviks. . . .

In the evening of November 6, Reed tells us, the Second All-Russian Congress of Soviets, as a sort of curtain raiser to the opening of the conference on the following day, held a prelimi-nary meeting in the Smolny assembly hall. "As night fell the great hall filled with soldiers and workmen, a monstrous dun mass, deep-humming in a blue haze of smoke." It was not until after midnight, however, that the meeting actually got under way. In deep silence Dan, the Menshevik leader, got up to speak, but an angry protest broke forth when, with his first words, he began to attack the Bolshevik rising. There was, Reed says,

> immense continued uproar, in which his voice could be heard screaming, as he pounded the desk, "Those who are urging this are committing a crime!" . . . Then for the Bolsheviks, Trotsky mounted the tribune, borne on a wave of roaring applause that burst into cheers and a rising house, thunderous. His thin pointed face was positively Mephistophelian in its expression of malicious irony. "Dan's tactics prove that the masses—the great, dull, indif-ferent masses—are absolutely with him!" (Titanic mirth). . . . "No. The history of the last seven months shows that the masses have left the Mensheviks. The Mensheviks and the Socialist Revolu-tionaries conquered the Cadets, and then when they got the power,

they gave it to the Cadets. . . . Dan tells you that you have no right to make an insurrection. Insurrection is the right of all revolutionists! When the downtrodden masses revolt, it is their right. . . ."

And so it went on: howls, shouts and catcalls as the rival speakers followed one another to the platform, until at last, sure of getting a majority at the opening of the Congress on the following day, the Bolsheviks walked out of the meeting.

Toward four in the morning (of November 7) Reed went into the outer hall of the building, and there met one of the Bolsheviks with a rifle slung from his shoulder.

> "We're moving," he said calmly but with satisfaction. "We pinched the assistant minister of justice and the minister of religions. They're down in the cellar now. One regiment is on the march to capture the telephone exchange, another the telegraph agency, another the state bank. The Red Guard is out. . . ."
>
> On the steps of Smolny, in the chill dark, we first saw the Red Guard—a huddled group of boys in workmen's clothes, carrying guns with bayonets, talking nervously together.
>
> Far over the still roofs westward came the sound of scattered rifle fire, where the yunkers were trying to open the bridges over the Neva, to prevent the factory workers and the soldiers of the Viborg quarter from joining the Soviet forces in the center of the city; and the Kronstadt sailors were closing them again. . . .
>
> Behind us great Smolny, bright with lights, hummed like a gigantic hive.

The Revolution Is Under Way

The events of the next twenty-four hours in Petrograd must surely be among the strangest in all Russian history. In the nature of things this should have been a day of terrible and serious drama, and so it was in many ways; and yet there was also a high, strained note of absurdity in much that happened, almost an element of farce. Philip Jordan, the American ambassador's Negro butler, perhaps summed it all up as well as anyone. In a letter he sent home to the United States he wrote, "On last Tuesday the Bolsheviks got the city in their hands and I want to tell you that it is something awful." By Tuesday (November 6) he meant Wednesday (November 7), but this does not matter in the least: "got the city in their hands" is perfect. It admirably conveys the infiltrating process, the stealthy almost accidental way in which the Bolsheviks pounced on one stronghold after another until like a house that has been eaten out by white ants, like a house of cards, the whole edifice of the government collapsed.

The people of Petrograd themselves were by no means fully aware of what was happening. Many of them went to work in the usual way on November 7; the shops stayed open, the streetcars ran, the movie theaters had their audiences, and the crowds were normal in the principal streets and except for the firing that broke out briefly in the evening, there was nothing much to show that this raw cold day marked the end of an era.

A good deal of the white-anting had been done during the night. By daybreak the Bolsheviks had seized the railway stations, the state bank, the power stations, the bridges across the river and finally the telephone exchange. Dawn disclosed that the cruiser *Aurora* was still in the Neva; with two torpedo boats she had come up to the Nicholas Bridge and had put ashore a party of sailors. There had been no resistance anywhere except for a few shots along the river, and the Cossack patrols were behaving with that air of appearing to notice nothing which usually overtakes policemen and soldiers who, in a crisis, are without leadership or definite orders.

Kerensky held an emergency cabinet meeting during the night and it was far from satisfactory; he appears to have suspected that Polkovnikov, instead of stamping out the rising, was deliberately allowing it to go forward so that he could eventually attempt a *coup d'état* of his own. Whether this was true or not it was now quite clear that reinforcements were needed, and during the morning Kerensky himself set off to find them. He hoped at Gatchina to rally the Third Cavalry Corps, that same corps which had served Kornilov [commander of the Petrograd garrison] so badly in September, and bring it into the city. However, nothing more was heard from Kerensky in the course of the day, and during his absence he lost the city. Once again, to use Sukhanov's [leader of the Mensheviks] phrase, "the break was accomplished with a sort of fabulous ease." It was even less eventful than the first rising in March.

At 10 A.M. on November 7 a proclamation was issued by Trotsky's Military Revolutionary Committee stating that the Provisional Government had fallen, and that power had passed to itself.

This was nothing more than a piece of political bluff, but it was rapidly becoming true, at any rate as far as Petrograd was concerned. The government ministers whom Kerensky had left in the Winter Palace were quite powerless. While they sat and debated one district after another went over to the Bolsheviks, and still the Cossacks did nothing. By midday it was apparent that there was nothing much they *could* do: almost all of the rest of the garrison was either neutral or actively supporting the rising, some twenty thousand Red Guards were in the streets, and a squadron of seven rebel warships was on the way from Kronstadt. In addition, several trainloads of armed sailors came in from Helsingfors in Finland, where the Bolshevik party was very strong.

The Pre-Parliament might have made a center of resistance, but it was outmaneuvered by simple violence; a gang of soldiers and sailors walked into the Mariinsky Palace with their rifles and ordered the delegates to disperse. The delegates had no course but to obey. After this the collapse became general, and by seven o'clock in the evening only the Winter Palace was holding out. Its position was precarious. Throughout the day there had been a steady stream of desertions from the garrison, and those that were left numbered barely a thousand, of whom 130 were women and the rest mainly officer cadets, an absurdly small force to hold a building that covered an area of 4½ acres. After Kerensky's departure for the front the thirteen remaining ministers in the government had continued in session in one of the rooms on the river side. They had dismissed Polkovnikov and had placed their faith instead in the expected arrival of loyal troops from outside the city. A direct wire connected the palace with General Dukhonin [commander and chief of Russian armies], who was now acting as chief of staff of the army at the front, and the general had sent reassuring messages in reply to the ministers' appeals for help. He had sounded out the political feeling in the armies along the front, and all except the northern army—that is to say, the one nearest to Petrograd—had declared that they would support the government. He promised that detachments of Cossacks and other reinforcements would soon arrive. Upon this the ministers decided to hold out. But they were not comfortable. Through the windows of their room they could see the rebel cruiser *Aurora* in the river, and the guns of St. Peter and St. Paul lay just beyond. By 6 P.M. the palace itself was invested by Bolshevik troops on every side, and artillery could be seen taking up positions in the main courtyard.

At 6:30 two messengers arrived from the Bolshevik forces with an ultimatum: either the ministers and their garrison must surrender within twenty minutes or the assault would begin. After a further consultation with Dukhonin on the teletype the ministers decided to continue their resistance. They removed themselves to a room in the interior of the building.

Two blank shots fired, one from the *Aurora*, the other from the Fortress of St. Peter and St. Paul, at 9 P.M. were the signal for action, and a desultory shelling of the palace began. It was not very effective—a few windows were smashed, a few stones were knocked down—but it was too much for the Women's Battalion. They came out to surrender and were soon followed by other deserters. Small parties of Red Guards now began to break into the outward rooms of the huge building, and those who did not become lost in the ornate corridors that stretched away like streets into the distance were engaged in a series of hand-to-hand skirmishes with the officer cadets. Neither side seems to have been very certain of itself: at one stage a Red Guard suddenly found himself confronted with the reflection of a painting of a horseman in a huge mirror, and with a horrified cry of "The Cavalry" he turned and bolted with his men. Huge crowds had gathered now in the Nevsky Prospekt, and all who could surged toward the palace. Armored cars with Bolshevik insignia daubed on their sides cruised about before the main entrance, but Reed and some friends with the aid of their American passports had no difficulty in getting into the building. The porters on duty at the door, wearing brass-buttoned uniforms with red and gold collars, politely took their coats.

After a pause of about an hour the shelling was resumed at 11 P.M. by the gunners in St. Peter and St. Paul, but not with much accuracy. No one was hurt. The psychological effects, however, were considerable. The slow solemn booming of the cannon seemed to many citizens to be an intolerable thing, and toward midnight the members of the Petrograd City Duma decided that they could stand it no longer. They carried a motion that they would march on the palace in a body and die with the Provisional Government; and in fact the mayor of the city, G.N. Schreider, armed with an umbrella and a lantern, did set out with a few followers. At the palace, however, Red sailors brusquely told them that they could not pass and eventually they returned to their homes.

At 1 A.M. on November 8 the last phase of the siege began. Red Guards began to infiltrate the corridors in earnest, and soon after two they rushed the inner room where the civilian ministers of the cabinet—the military members had already surrendered—were meeting. These men, who had behaved with some courage and dignity throughout the day, were arrested and taken off to the dungeons of St. Peter and St. Paul. Casualties caused by the whole operation hardly amounted to twenty men and none of the defenders were seriously hurt.

While these events were going on the conspirators at Smolny had had a momentous day. Lenin had appeared at a meeting of the Petrograd Soviet in the afternoon—a rapturous moment for his followers—and Trotsky had announced triumphantly that the revolution was proving bloodless. Telegrams had been sent off to the front announcing the fall of the government. . . .

Opposition to the Bolsheviks

The Bolsheviks were by no means secure as yet. No reply had been received to the telegrams which Trotsky had sent out to the army, and it was still entirely possible that the soldiers would not acknowledge this revolution. No one had any news of what Kerensky was doing. It was simply rumored that he had mustered a force that was now marching on the city. Even inside Petrograd itself the opposition was recovering from its initial surprise; a Committee for the Salvation of the Country and the Revolution was being formed, and it had the support of all the right-wing elements, all the moderates, all those who might normally have remained neutral but now detested the Bolsheviks because of the violence that was being done at the Winter Palace. . . .

A curious stillness settled on Petrograd during the remaining hours of darkness. On this of all nights no holdups or robberies occurred, and except for the continuous commotion at Smolny no move of any consequence was made by either side. Bright searchlights played on the walls of the Winter Palace, and a mob of soldiers tramped through the halls and corridors within, but there was no further disturbance. In the morning, Sukhanov says, the newspapers came out as usual, most of the editorials thundering against the Bolsheviks. But there was very little news in them. . . .

By midday, however, certain definite information was available and it was important. A bicycle battalion which had been advancing on the city to defend the government—and at this stage one battalion might have made all the difference—had halted and had come over to the Bolsheviks. In Moscow the garrison had risen against the government. And from the front there was a message to say that the Twelfth Army supported the rising. All this was great encouragement for Smolny; indeed, when the news about the Twelfth Army came in pandemonium broke out and the delegates flung their arms round one another, weeping with relief.

But there was bad news for the Bolsheviks as well, and it came chiefly from the worst possible quarter, from the workers themselves. The Union of Railway Workers declared that it was opposed to the Bolshevik coup and demanded that the new government should be a coalition of all the socialist parties. The union also threatened to tie up the whole railroad system of Russia if the Bolsheviks precipitated a civil war. This was a serious threat, and it was all the more serious because the post and telegraph workers had also announced their opposition to the Bolsheviks. A general strike began to spread through all the government departments. Inside Smolny Lenin and Trotsky spent most of this day, Thursday, November 8, in rallying those weaker elements in the Congress and inside their own party who were beginning to think that some sort of compromise ought to be patched up with the moderate socialist groups. But it was with the army that both Lenin and Trotsky were most deeply concerned; with the army on their side their cause was won, without it they were finished. Appeal after appeal went out to the Cossacks, to the city garrisons and to the front-line regiments, urging the soldiers to acknowledge the fall of the government. . . .

At 8:40 on the evening of November 8 the Congress assembled for another meeting, and this time Lenin himself went onto the platform with the presidium. There was the usual commotion, and at last Lenin got up to speak. He stood there, says Reed, "gripping the edge of the reading stand, letting his little winking eyes travel over the crowd . . . apparently oblivious to the long-rolling ovation, which lasted several minutes. When it finished he said simply, 'We shall now proceed to construct the Socialist order.' Again that overwhelming human roar."

Trotsky does not remember Lenin uttering that lapidary phrase about the socialist order, but it seems hardly likely that Reed could have invented it; and in fact the words indicated precisely

what Lenin now proceeded to do, except that it was Lenin himself who did the constructing in his own fashion and not the over-
wrought delegates, who stood jammed in the body of the hall.
He read a proclamation. There was to be peace, immediate peace,
peace without annexations or indemnities. The secret treaties
with the Allies were to be repudiated and the self-determination
of peoples was to be guaranteed.

It was a proposition that could hardly fail to please the meeting, and when it was approved by a unanimous vote something
like delirium seized the crowd. Sobbing, with shining eyes, they
sang the "Internationale," and when someone cried, "The war is
ended," it really seemed to be true. There was another shout,
"Remember dead comrades," and this was the signal for the
singing of the Funeral March.

Lenin continued impassively. His next proposal was that the
meeting should approve of a decree by which all private owner-
ship of land in Russia was abolished. No compensation was to
be paid to the landowners. This also was put to the vote and after a long debate was passed with only one dissenting voice. . . .

Friday, November 9, the third day of the rising, was the beginning of an awakening throughout Russia. By now the news of
the happenings in the capital had spread to the more remote
towns and military garrisons, and a vast debate was going on: to
support the rising or oppose it, to go over to the Bolsheviks or
join the Committee for Salvation? Everywhere men began to
drift into one or other of these two camps, and a stream of propaganda poured out from the rival headquarters. It was not easy
for the *moujik* or the illiterate soldier to make up his mind. Reed
describes one typical meeting that took place at the Mikhailovsky
Riding School in Petrograd. Two thousand men of an armored
car regiment which up to now had remained neutral were gathered in a compact mass around one of their vehicles which
served as a platform. Under a single arc light speaker after
speaker got up to put the opposing sides of the case. "Never,"
Reed says, "have I seen men trying so hard to understand, to decide. They never moved, stood staring with a sort of terrible in-
tentness at the speaker. . . ." In this case it was the Bolsheviks
who won the day—Krylenko, a new commissar for military affairs, managed to swing the meeting—but it was not so among
the civil servants in Petrograd. The employees in most of the
ministries came out on strike, and both the railwaymen and the

post and telegraph staff remained adamant. Nor was it so in Moscow, where loyal troops struck back at the insurgents in the Kremlin and forced them to surrender. . . .

Final Victory

The next three days were a period of continuous suspense in Petrograd. It was now known that Kerensky had joined General Krasnov, and with a force of Cossacks was advancing on Tsarskoe Selo. In actual fact this force of Cossacks numbered only seven hundred men, but no one knew that in Petrograd and fantastic rumors flew about. A whole army was said to be bearing down on the city, and there was a rush to dig trenches and to throw up barricades in the streets. It was hoped that Kerensky would be stopped in the open plains to the south of the capital, and a force of Red Guards and sailors had gone out to do battle there, somewhat in the manner of General Gallieni, who had saved Paris from the Germans at the beginning of the war: anyone who wanted to fight went off, cars and cabs were grabbed by the soldiers off the streets, volunteers manned the locomotives of the troop trains, and there was an atmosphere of desperate resolution about it all. But would they succeed? Even at Smolny the comrades were beginning to ask, "What chance has a mob got against trained soldiers?"

On November 11 fighting broke out again in the city. It was a short but extremely savage affair; a group of officer cadets rushed the telephone exchange (which meant that Smolny was cut off once more), and all day went by before the Red forces could get them out. This time there were something over one hundred casualties. The situation was even more serious for the Bolsheviks in Moscow; after a short armistice heavy fighting had begun again, and the government forces still dominated the Kremlin. . . .

Trotsky in his reminiscences is perfectly frank about the danger that threatened the Bolsheviks through these three days: it was touch and go. With every day that went by more and more people were gathering around the Committee of Salvation, and from the banks the Committee had all the money it wanted. The weather turned cold and gloomy with a touch of snow in the air, and through the long dark hours there was now one overriding thought in everybody's mind: when will Kerensky come?

It was not until Tuesday, November 13, that this state of tension was broken. Trotsky himself had gone to the front, and it was he who sent the news. "The night of November 12/13," he wired to Smolny, "will go down in history. . . . Kerensky . . . has been decisively repulsed. Kerensky is retreating. We are advancing. . . ." There had been a short battle at Tsarskoe Selo but the Cossacks, like almost everyone else in this revolution of words, had succumbed to the speeches of the Bolshevik agitators; they had agreed to negotiate and that was as good as a victory. Petrograd was saved. A great wave of relief swept over the Council of People's Commissars at Smolny. . . .

For the moment . . . the Bolsheviks in Petrograd were secure, or at any rate secure enough to reject the pressure on them to form a coalition government with the other socialist parties. With the defeat of Kerensky all negotiations on that score came to an end. On November 15 the government forces in the Kremlin surrendered; the Bolsheviks shelled them out of their last stronghold in the arsenal, and with this all serious opposition in Moscow collapsed.

Heavy snow had begun to fall, and there was a bright and sparkling quality in the air. To the more poetical Bolsheviks it was a symbol of their inner joy. They had had an unbelievable success. Not much more than a week had elapsed since Lenin with his bandage around his face had come secretly into Smolny to urge them into action, and now they had usurped an empire.

The Legacy of World War I

by John Steele Gordon

John Steele Gordon is a columnist and author. His column, "The Business of America," has appeared in *American Heritage* while his books have examined historical and economic subjects: *The Great Game* (the history of Wall Street), *Hamilton's Blessing* (the story of the national debt), and *A Thread Across the Ocean* (the saga of the trans-Atlantic cable). As a general way to see the significance of World War I, Gordon's analysis is worthwhile. He explores in the following piece how the war influenced world events. But, more importantly, he shows how the great struggle caused Western civilization to question many of the values it had held; the war inflicted a severe psychological trauma to the world. He ends with an important discussion of four lessons the war has taught us.

The diplomat and historian George Kennan called it "the seminal catastrophe of the twentieth century": the First World War.

Certainly that war's influence on subsequent world events could hardly have been more pervasive. Had there been no First World War, there would, of course, have been no Second, and that is not just playing with numbers, for in geopolitical terms the two wars were really one with a twenty-year truce in the middle.

But for the First World War, the sun might still shine brightly on the British Empire. But for the war, there would have been no Bolshevik coup and thus no Soviet state. But for the war, there would have been no Nazis and thus no genocide of the Jews.

And, of course, most of us never would have been born. . . . The First World War, more than any other in history, was psychologically debilitating, both for the vanquished and for the victors. Indeed, there really was no victory. No premeditated policy of conquest or revenge brought the war about—although both those aims had clouded the politics of Europe for years. Therefore, no aims, beyond national survival, were achieved.

Indeed, relations among the Great Powers of Europe were better in the early summer of 1914 than they had been for some time. The British and Germans had recently agreed about the Berlin to Baghdad railway and a future division between them of Portugal's colonies. Even the French, still bitter over their ignominious defeat at the hands of Prussia in 1871, were moving to improve relations with Germany, a move that Germany welcomed.

Rather, the war came about because a lunatic murdered a man of feathers and uniforms who had no real importance whatsoever. The politicians, seeking to take advantage of circumstances—as politicians are paid to do—had then miscalculated in their blustering and posturing.

The mobilization of an army when railroads were the only means of mass transportation was a very complex undertaking, one that had to be planned in advance down to the smallest detail. Once a mobilization plan was implemented, it could not be stopped without throwing a country's military into chaos, rendering it largely defenseless. Russia, seeking only to threaten Austria and thus prevent its using the assassination of Archduke Ferdinand to stir up trouble in the Balkans, discovered that it could not move just against Austria. It was general mobilization or nothing. Russia chose to mobilize.

At that point the statesmen realized that the war they had threatened so freely—but which no one, in fact, had wanted at all—had now, suddenly, become inescapable. A fearful, inexorable logic had taken decisions out of human hands.

Once it began, the generals found they had no tactical concepts to deal with the new military realities that confronted them. It had been forty-three years since Great Powers had fought each other in Europe. In those four decades the instruments of war had undergone an unparalleled evolution, and their destructive power had increased by several orders of magnitude.

Railroads, machine guns, and barbed wire made an entrenched defense invulnerable. Stalemate—bloody, endless, gloryless stalemate—resulted. For lack of any better ideas, the generals flung greater and greater numbers of men into the mouths of these machine guns and gained at best mere yards of territory thereby.

In the first day—day!—of the Battle of the Somme in 1916, Great Britain suffered twenty thousand men killed. That was the bloodiest day in the British army's long history. Altogether there were more than a million casualties in this one battle alone. An entire generation was lost in the slaughter of the Somme and other similar battles.

This almost unimaginable destruction of human life, to no purpose whatsoever, struck at the very vitals of Western society. For this reason alone, among the casualties of the First World War were not only the millions of soldiers who had died for nothing, most of the royalty of Europe, and treasure beyond reckoning but nearly all the fundamental philosophical and cultural assumptions of the civilization that had suffered this self-induced catastrophe.

For there was one thing that was immediately clear to all about the Great War—as the generation who fought it called it—and that was that this awful tragedy was a human and wholly local phenomenon. There was no volcano, no wrathful God, no horde of barbarians out of the East. Western culture had done this to itself. Because of the war, it seemed to many a matter of inescapable logic that Western culture must be deeply, inherently flawed. . . .

Attitude of the West Before the War

At the end of the nineteenth century, any comparison between the West and other cultures bordered on the meaningless, so great had the gap in power and wealth grown. Westerners had projected that power over the entire globe and created the modern world, a world they utterly dominated. The Western people of that world took for granted what seemed to them the manifest superiority of Western technology, governance, and even religion over all others.

To better understand the predominant attitudes of the West before the First World War, consider what it accomplished in the nineteenth century as a result of the Industrial Revolution. Quite simply, the quality of life was miraculously transformed. Indoor plumbing, central heating, brilliant interior lighting, abundant clothing, and myriad inexpensive industrial products from wallpaper to iceboxes gave the middle and upper classes a standard of living undreamed of a century earlier by even the richest members of society.

In 1800 it had required a month to cross the Atlantic in a damp, crowded, and pitching ship. In 1900 vast and luxurious liners made the crossing in a week. Information that once had been limited to the speed of human travel could now circle the entire globe in minutes by telephone, telegraph, and undersea cable.

In the 1830s the lights and shadows of an instant were captured by photography. In the 1870s Edison's phonograph imprisoned sound. To the Victorians it was as though time itself had been tamed.

Newspapers, books, and magazines proliferated by the thousands so that information and entertainment could be quickly and cheaply obtained. Free public libraries spread to nearly every city in the Western world. Andrew Carnegie alone paid for nearly five thousand of them in the United States and Britain.

Physics, chemistry, geology, and biology penetrated farther into the fathomless heart of nature than anyone had thought possible a hundred years earlier. Even the mighty Newton's model of the universe was found to be less than wholly universal when Einstein published his Special Theory of Relativity in 1905.

As the new century began engineers showed the world with the Crystal Palace in London how to enclose vast spaces, with the Brooklyn Bridge in New York how to span great distances, with the Eiffel Tower in Paris how to scale great heights. The automobile, the airplane, the movies, and wireless communication promised still more wonders. . . .

Who can blame the people who accomplished all this for feeling good about themselves? Would we, or anyone, have been any wiser or more humble?

Because of this fantastic record of progress . . . people . . . believed in the inevitability of further progress and the certainty that science would triumph. They believed in the ever-widening spread of democracy and the rule of law. They believed in the adequacy of the present and the bright promise of the future. To be sure, they fought ferociously over the details of how to proceed, but they had no doubt whatever that the basic principles that guided their society were correct.

Then, all at once, the shots rang out in Sarajevo, the politicians bungled, the armies marched, the poppies began to blow between the crosses row on row. The faith of the Western world in the soundness of its civilization died in the trenches of the western front.

Seventy-five years later, richer, more powerful, more learned than ever, the West still struggles to pick up the psychological pieces, to regain its poise, to find again the self-confidence that in the nineteenth century it took entirely for granted. . . .

Lessons of the War

All this is not to say that there was nothing to be learned from the First World War and its terrible consequences, that it was all just a ghastly aberration. I think that we . . . have learned at least four vital lessons from the catastrophe.

Before the war Westerners believed not only in the superiority of Western culture but in the innate superiority of the white race over what many, twisting Kipling's meaning, referred to as those "lesser breeds without the Law." Today no one but the hopeless bigot believes that those who could inflict the Battle of Verdun upon themselves are a special creation or the sole repository of human genius. The Great War taught us that all human beings are equally human: equally frail and equally sublime.

The second lesson of the First World War was to hammer home forever the truth first uttered by William Tecumseh Sherman thirty-five years earlier. "I am tired and sick of war," the great general said in 1879. "Its glory is all moonshine. . . . War is hell." At 11:00 A.M., on November 11, 1918, as the guns fell silent after fifty-one months and 8,538,315 military deaths, there was hardly a soul on earth who would have disagreed with him. Nor are there many today. If wars have been fought since, they have been fought by people who suffered few illusions about war's glory.

The third lesson is that in a technological age, war between the Great Powers cannot be won in anything but a Pyrrhic sense. In the stark phraseology of the accountant, war is no longer even remotely cost-effective.

The final lesson is that it is very easy in a technological age for war to become inevitable. The speed with which war is fought has increased manyfold since the Industrial Revolution began. In 1914 the Austrians, the Russians, and the German kaiser rattled one too many sabers, and suddenly, much to their surprise, the lights began to go out all over Europe. This all too vividly demonstrated fact has induced considerable caution in the world's statesmen ever since—if not, alas, in its madmen.

Bearing this in mind, there is one aspect of the First World War for which we might be grateful: If it had to be fought, it was well that it was fought when it was. We learned the lessons of total war in a technological age less than forty years before we developed the capacity to destroy ourselves utterly with this technology. Had the political situation that led to the Great War coincided with the technological possibilities that produced the hydrogen bomb, it is improbable that there would have been a Tom Wolfe's New York—or even any New Yorkers to look back and wonder what happened to Edith Wharton's.

Rather, the great metropolis, a city humming with human life and human genius, would instead be but one more pile of rubble on a vast and desolate plain, poisoned for centuries. If we have truly learned this final lesson, and we must pray that we have, then those millions who lie today in Flanders fields did not die in vain.

The Treaty of Versailles Is Signed

by Charles L. Mee Jr.

The author of the following excerpt, Charles L. Mee Jr., was formerly the editor at *Horizon* magazine and author of several successful books, including *Meeting at Potsdam* and *Seizure*. In the following book excerpt, he discusses the signing of the Treaty of Versailles, which officially ended the horrible carnage of World War I.

The treaty came about because of the collapse of Germany and its allies in late 1918. America had entered the war, and the Allies, consisting primarily of France, Great Britain, and the United States, took the offensive on the battlefield. Turkey and other smaller members of Germany's alliance signed armistices in September and October. Next, Austria-Hungary fell apart—the Hungarians, Czechs, Slovaks, and Poles declared their independence from the former ally of Germany. Finally, elements of the German military rebelled against their leaders even though the fighting had not yet reached German territory. Food and supplies dwindled in Germany as the Allied blockade choked the economic life of its enemy. In desperation, the German general Paul von Hindenburg told Kaiser Wilhelm II, the ruler of Germany, to seek an immediate armistice. On November 11, 1918, the war finally came to a close.

In January 1919 delegates from the victorious countries met in Paris, France, to begin work on a formal treaty. The leaders who played the crucial roles were David Lloyd George of England,

Georges Clemenceau of France, and Woodrow Wilson of the United States. For six months they labored with conflicting goals to hammer out a treaty. The final form of the treaty set forth several key points—it blamed Germany alone for the outbreak of the war, stripped Germany of much territory, set extremely high reparations that Germany was forced to pay, disarmed Germany, and called for the establishment of a League of Nations to maintain peace in the world.

It was a bitter pill for the Germans to swallow, but they had little choice since their nation could no longer carry on the war against overwhelming numbers. So, on June 28, 1919, a signing ceremony was held in the Hall of Mirrors of the historic palace of Versailles, built near Paris by King Louis XIV in the late 1600s. The following excerpt gives a brief summary of the war's devastation, explains what happened on the day the treaty was signed, and explores the significance of the treaty for the world.

World War I had been a tragedy on a dreadful scale. Sixty-five million men were mobilized—more by many millions than had ever been brought to war before—to fight a war, they had been told, of justice and honor, of national pride and of great ideals, to wage a war that would end all war, to establish an entirely new order of peace and equity in the world.

But far from resolving the conflicts that had begun the war, the war had let loose even more turmoil. By November 11, 1918, when the armistice that marked the end of the war was signed, eight million soldiers lay dead, twenty million more were wounded, diseased, mutilated, or spitting blood from the gas attacks. Twenty-two million civilians had been killed or wounded, and the survivors were living in villages blasted to splinters and rubble, on farms churned to mud, their cattle dead.

In Berlin and Belgrade and Petrograd, the survivors fought among themselves—fourteen wars, great or small, civil or revolutionary, flickered or raged about the world. Thirteen million tons of shipping had been sunk; 10,000 square miles of northern France had been ruined; 1,200 churches were destroyed along with 250,000 other buildings. Hundreds of square miles of central and Eastern Europe were in even worse condition. In Poland, people traded with German marks, Austrian krönen, Polish marks that had been issued by the Germans, Russian rubles—all plagued by uncertain exchange rates and runaway inflation. Prices rose in Austria by a factor of 14,000, in Hungary by 23,000, in Poland by 2,500,000, and in Russia by 400,000,000. And people starved all across Europe.

In central Europe, a member of a relief commission reported that "in countries where I found wagons I found . . . a shortage of locomotives; where there were locomotives, there was a shortage of wagons; where coal lay at the pithead . . . there were no wagons and where wagons waited, men were not available to work the coal. . . . In many parts of Poland, children were dying for want of milk and adults were unable to obtain bread or fats. In eastern districts . . . the population was living on roots, grass, acorns, and heather." Those who managed to survive the war and the revolutions and the violence and the privations were stunned by an epidemic of influenza that struck and spread and struck and spread again in the last spasm of the war and killed yet another six million people.

Four great empires had fallen—the German, Austro-Hungarian, Turkish or Ottoman, and the Russian—and the Allied armies still fought on in Russia against the Bolsheviks, trying vainly to restore the White Russians to rule. The collapse of these empires gave birth to the great political drama that commenced at the Paris Peace Conference and continues to rage today: the conflict among the major powers to move into the old imperial domains—and the struggle of the other nations to win independence altogether from imperialism.

Perhaps all of this turmoil could have been contained had the political collapse not occurred in the midst of a collapse of many of the traditional ideals and usages that had underlain the political order of the nineteenth century. But the war had discredited much of the rhetoric of national pride, honor, and sacrifice, as well as faith in the notions of reason, progress, humanism. Nor did the notions of God, representational art, or Newtonian physics appear to be in such good repair. The "modern" western civilization that had grown up since the Renaissance was under siege from outside, and from within, and offered scant support to the disintegrating political order.

By January of 1919, as the delegates gathered in Paris for the Peace Conference, the shallow graves of Verdun were being washed out by the rains; feet stuck out of the ground, and helmets with skulls in them rose up through the mud. In this atmosphere, the diplomats gathered—and, far from restoring order to the world, they took the chaos of the Great War, and, through vengefulness and inadvertence, impotence and design, they sealed it as the permanent condition of our century. . . .

The end [of the war] came on Saturday, June 28. By noon the road to Versailles was jammed with automobiles, most of them with large colored labels on their hoods and windshields. At the intersection of the Avenue de Picardie and Boulevard de la Reine, the cars with tricolor or yellow and green cockades were directed straight down the avenue, while all other cars were sent down the boulevard. Then at the intersection of the Avenue de St.-Cloud and Rue St.-Pierre, the cars with the tricolor were directed along the Rue St.-Pierre to the Avenue de Paris and on to the front of the palace, where troops in horizon-blue uniforms lined the avenues into the courtyard. Inside the courtyard were the cavalry with their pennants of red and white and the Garde Républicaine in white breeches, white crossbelts, burnished crested helmets with long black and red horsehair crinière, black riding boots, swords at rest in front of them. The limousines pulled up in the forecourt before the entrance to the marble staircase. General Pershing was among the first to arrive, followed by Secretary Lansing, General Manoury, who had been blinded in the war and who was helped from his limousine by General Alby, then the maharajah of Bikaner, Baron Makino, M. Antoine Dubost, wearing the medal of 1870 on his chest, and then, at last, arriving with General Mordacq, Clemenceau, greeted with sudden shouts and cheers, Lloyd George applauded by the attendants in the marble court, and President and Mrs. Wilson, also applauded as they stepped from their limousine to mount the stairway up into the palace and through the apartments of Marie Antoinette. The palace looked, on this day, especially ostentatious. . . .

When, at last, the diplomats entered the Hall of Mirrors, 240 feet long, 35 feet wide, 42 feet high, designed by Mansart in 1678, they were thrust into a pandemonium amid the gold gilt, the frieze of little allegorical figures of children and trophies of war, the paintings of Louis le Grand on the ceiling, the great wall of seventeen windows opening into the gardens, and the facing wall of seventeen vast mirrors reflecting all these diplomats, Louis le Grand, allegorical children, journalists, eight-branched silver candelabra decorated with the labors of Hercules, Lloyd

George's special contingent of fifty disabled soldiers, two grubby old men—country friends of Clemenceau's—in special chairs in the center of the spectacle, secretaries, photographers, colonels, "a mass of little humans," said the painter William Orpen, "all trying to get to different places." Sir Henry Wilson estimated the crowd at "about 1,000 people, of whom I daresay 150 were ladies, which I thought all wrong."

Along the mirrored side of the vast hall was a long horseshoe table. At the center of the horseshoe table was the place reserved for Clemenceau. To his left were chairs for the delegates from Britain, the Dominions, and Japan. To his right were chairs for the representatives from the United States, France, Italy, Belgium. Chairs for the delegations of the other nations were arrayed around the horseshoe; the reporters had already learned that the chairs reserved for the Chinese would not be occupied.

In front of this long table "like a guillotine," said Nicolson, was the table on which the treaty of peace lay to be signed. The treaty existed in only one official copy, printed with a wide margin on Japanese vellum and held together with red tape. The personal seals of the signatories had already been affixed to the document, in order to save time, so that the delegates would only need to sign their names next to their seals.

Tapestry-covered backless benches had been put out for seating and the delegates clustered in the aisles, pushed by one another, and stepped over the benches as they moved about the room trying to collect autographs on their programs. Almost everyone agreed that the French had arranged the room badly, and Mrs. Wilson had to content herself on a backless bench until someone filched an armchair for her. The accommodations for the press, Lord Riddell said, were "very much like a bear garden."

At about two forty-five o'clock, Clemenceau moved purposefully through the crowd and took his seat at the center of the horseshoe table. He was followed almost at once by President Wilson, who attracted a small flurry of polite applause, and then by Lloyd George, who took his place at the long table. Clemenceau made a gesture to the ushers, who commenced to say "Ssh! Ssh!" as they moved up and down the aisles. The diplomats took their seats quickly; the chattering subsided; an occasional cough or throat-clearing could be heard in the hall, the rustle of programs, a short military order followed by the sound of the swords of the Garde Républicaine being returned smartly to their scabbards, and then the crisp order of Clemenceau breaking the silence: "Faîtes entrer les Allemands."

"I suppose, now," Balfour had said several days before, "[the Germans will] send us a few bow-legged, cross-eyed men to sign the treaty." In fact, Dr. Hermann Müller and Dr. Johannes Bell—the secretary for foreign affairs and the colonial secretary, respectively, of the new German government—were deathly pale and kept their eyes fixed on the ceiling as they entered the Hall of Mirrors, in order to avoid the stares of the assembled company. None of the delegates of the Allied powers stood to receive the Germans. . . .

Dr. Müller, a tall man with a little black moustache, and Dr. Bell, round-faced and uncomfortable, bowed, and took their seats—their legs shaking uncontrollably once they sat down—next to the small table holding the treaty. Clemenceau spoke briefly and without pleasantries:

A crowd watches as the Treaty of Versailles is signed on June 28, 1919, at the Hall of Mirrors in France.

"An agreement has been reached upon the conditions of the treaty of peace. . . . The signatures about to be given constitute an irrevocable engagement to carry out loyally and faithfully in their entirety all the conditions that have been decided upon. I therefore have the honor of asking messieurs the German plenipotentiaries to approach to affix their signatures to the treaty before me."

The Germans leapt up to sign the treaty and were motioned to sit down again while Mantoux translated Clemenceau's speech into German. Then the Germans rose again and stepped forward to sign the document. The pen did not work. Colonel House stepped forward with a pen. Dr. Bell, either out of nervousness or haste, omitted his Christian name and signed in a heavy, perpendicular script, "Dr. Bell."

The five American commissioners signed next, led by the president. In moving Wilson's personal library from Princeton to the White House, one of his aides noticed that Wilson had tried out various inscriptions—Thomas W. Wilson, Thomas Woodrow Wilson, T.W. Wilson, T. Woodrow Wilson—before settling on Woodrow Wilson as his customary signature. The president realized he was excited when, after writing "Woodrow" with perfect ease, he had some difficulty signing "Wilson."

Wilson was followed by Lansing, House, Bliss, and White; Lloyd George was followed by Balfour, Lord Milner, Bonar Law. Clemenceau was followed by Pichon, Klotz, Tardieu, and Cambon. Then came the delegations of Italy, Japan, Belgium, and the others. The ceremony moved along with surprising swiftness—and, as the delegates formed a line in front of the signature table, conversations started up, the buzz of voices filled the hall, and a casual feeling pervaded the room as the delegates chatted with one another.

Riddell was appalled by the bad management, the sense of informality, the feeling of disorder that overtook the ceremony of the signing. Lloyd George noticed, to his disgust, that delegates were actually going up to the Germans and asking for their autographs. The more squeamish among the American and British delegates were overcome with a sense of shame that the ceremony seemed to subject the Germans to unnecessary humiliation. Nicolson pronounced the whole messy affair "horrible."

As soon as the Germans had signed the treaty, a signal was sent out to the gun battery of St.-Cyr on the southern slopes of

Versailles, and the firing of the cannon was taken up by one fort after another on the hills around Paris; the waiting crowds had begun to cheer—and so, as the chatting delegates continued the signing, their signatures were accompanied by the muffled cheers and the booming of the cannon.

When the last of the signatures had been placed on the treaty, the last pen put down on the table, Clemenceau closed the session abruptly. ("Messieurs, all the signatures have been given. The signature of the conditions of peace between the Allied and associated powers and the German republic is an accomplished fact. The session is adjourned.")

The Germans rose and vanished from the hall at once through a side door; the delegates milled about to congratulate one another. Through the windows, past the terrace, the fountains could be seen: bright sunlight, open country, clear blue sky, white clouds, a squadron of airplanes in the sky, a cordon of troops holding back the crowds in the gardens. Wilson made his way through the throng of delegates; Lloyd George shook hands, smiling; Clemenceau walked among the milling diplomats, shaking hands, his eyes bleary, saying, "Oui, c'est une belle journée."

Wilson, Lloyd George, and Clemenceau appeared together out on the terrace, and the crowd burst into cheers, arms waving, car horns joining in with the booming of the cannon, well-wishers grasping the hands of the Big Three, thumping them on their backs as they wandered out onto the grass, and Wilson, finally, reached out to take Clemenceau's hand, because the old man, on this, his day of triumph, relief, and dismay, did not seem to know where he was going, and his eyes were filled with tears. . . .

The Results

When all the diplomats had dispersed at last, and the Palace of Versailles was left to the gardeners, and the delegations returned once more to their homelands, the Europe that they left behind still trembled with the wounds and shocks of war and the insults of peace.

A generation had been decimated on the battlefields of Europe. No one had seen the likes of such slaughter before: the deaths of soldiers per day of battle were 10 times greater than in the American Civil War, 24 times the deaths in the Napoleonic Wars, 550 times the deaths in the Boer War. And still the epidemic of flu spread through Europe and America and elsewhere until it had claimed another 14 million lives among the survivors of the war.

The economy of Europe was in ruins. Food prices had risen during the war by 103 percent in Rome, by 106 percent in Paris, by 110 percent in London, and, in Germany, prices had become all but meaningless. The Germans had 40 percent less butter than in 1914, 42 percent less meat, 50 percent less milk. The destruction of factories, railroads, and shipping produced economic dislocation on such an order as to be excruciating.

Even before the treaty had been signed, the so-called Vilna dispute had erupted into a pocket war. The Polish general Joseph Pilsudski took the town of Vilna from the Bolsheviks; diplomatic negotiations returned the town to the Bolsheviks—who only had it taken from them by the Lithuanians who were driven out by a band of Polish freebooters.

The Teschen conflict, too, commenced before the Paris conference had adjourned, and then the Polish-Russian War broke out, and then the Burgenland dispute between Austria and Hungary over a strip of territory predominantly inhabited by Germans but occupied by Hungarian irregulars and assigned by the peace conference to Austria.

On June 22, 1920, Greece, encouraged by Lloyd George, invaded Anatolia, and Turkey invaded Armenia. In Italy, Gabriele d'Annunzio led an expedition into Fiume. The Italians negotiated with the Yugoslavs and gave up Fiume—but a Fascist coup overthrew the government and forced Yugoslavia to abandon its claims.

Anxiety led to the formation of the kind of interlocking set of alliances in which the world had been caught in 1914. In February of 1920, France and Poland signed a pact to come to one another's assistance in case of attack; in March of 1920, Poland and Rumania signed a defense treaty. Several weeks later, Germany was said to be in default on some of its war debts; the French occupied Düsseldorf, Duisburg, and Ruhrort. In April, Rumania joined Czechoslovakia in the Little Entente.

The war had cost $603.57 billion. Rubber was in such short supply in Europe that trucks were traveling on their rims, and fats were so scarce that housewives strained their dishwater to salvage whatever grease it might contain. International trade was in shambles: British exports were only half what they had been before the war. By 1921, the world economy had stumbled into a brief, but portentous, depression, distinguished not by uniformity but by apparent caprice. While the manufacture of gas masks and airplane wings ceased, the production of copper and wheat continued at such vigorous wartime levels that prices slumped precipitately.

And then inflation struck. In Germany, to pay for the war, the money in circulation had been quintupled; public debt was 20 times its prewar level. The exchange was 4 marks to the dollar in 1914, then 14.8 marks to the dollar in May of 1921, then 62.6 marks to the dollar in November of 1921, and then 62 *billion* marks to the dollar in October of 1923. . . .

At the conclusion of the Paris conference, Wilson returned from Europe to do battle with the United States Senate over ratification of the treaty. Colonel House had advised the president, just before Wilson sailed for America, to be conciliatory to his Senate opponents. Of ninety-six senators, only fourteen Republicans and four Democrats were unalterably opposed to the treaty—and the majority of American citizens favored its adoption. But, before Wilson boarded the *George Washington* he said to the colonel: "House, I have found one can never get anything in this life that is worthwhile without fighting for it.". . .

As for the treaty itself, it was rejected by the Congress of the United States. It was formally accepted by the French, but only grudgingly, and was pilloried, beginning at once and continuously, by both the left and the right. Formally accepted by the English, the treaty was savaged at once by Keynes in his book *The Economic Consequences of the Peace*, which set off a sustained attack on the treaty by English liberals. English shame over the treaty provisions encouraged the Germans, increasingly, to believe that they could ignore or violate it with impunity. The treaty was despised in Germany, hated by the Japanese, not signed by the Chinese, and it was the subject of denunciatory expositions in school classrooms in Hungary, Austria, Yugoslavia, and the rest of Eastern Europe.

Through all this, Hitler rose to power. He made his first public impression, and he continued to draw audiences, and hold and augment them, by delivering the same speech over and over again: a vitriolic speech entitled "The Treaty of Versailles."

No single conclusion can be drawn from all this disaster without diminishing the experience of history itself. The lesson of Versailles is protean, not simple, and as the event is turned over in the mind, a hundred different nuances and shadings appear. The experience cannot be impaled on one moral or another. Yet, certain lessons suggest themselves with an undeniable insistence.

The first, surely, is a reminder of the double maxim: it is always easier to start a war than to end one, let alone win it. And the second is that harshness and vengeance nearly always return to haunt those who impose them.

But of all the lessons that Versailles leaves us, certainly the most insistent is that of the inability of the few any longer to govern the many. The few world rulers who dominated Versailles simply could not any longer settle the fate of the many new nations. The few old imperial powers could no longer impose their will on the many new peoples who took their destinies into their own hands. The few heads of state gathered in a small room could no longer determine the world in which we live.

The failure of the diplomats of 1919—a failure that no one has since been able to repair, whose results we have lived with ever since—has been a terribly mixed legacy. The rise of Hitler, the Second World War, the riots and revolutions that plague a world without political order have been the cause of enormous bloodshed and suffering. Yet, at the same time, the collapse of the old order was a necessary prelude to the spread of self-rule, the liberation of new nations and classes, the release of new freedom and independence. The old order was, finally, an ally of old privilege, a fossil of the nineteenth century, a relic of a clockwork universe that had gone out of existence forever.

Aftermath of the Treaty: The League of Nations Provides a Model for Global Cooperation

by E.H. Carr

E.H. Carr was a political scientist and historian. He held various positions in his adult life—a diplomat, a professor of international relations in Wales, and an assistant editor of the London *Times*. In the following selection, he discusses the successes of the League of Nations, which came about because of the Treaty of Versailles. Most people today think only of the failure of the league to prevent the aggressions of Adolf Hitler and Benito Mussolini, but it had many small successes between its inception in 1919 and its breakdown in the 1930s. The League of Nations settled disputes, heard grievances of various minorities throughout the world, administered the Saar territory, provided ways for international economic cooperation, improved working conditions worldwide, and set up a court of international justice. In addition, it helped create the atmosphere that led to

E.H. Carr, *International Relations Between the Two World Wars, 1919–1939*. New York: Harper & Row, 1947.

a global renunciation of war that continues to echo today in such
bodies as the United Nations.

The principal business of the League was, and was bound to
remain, the prevention of war by the peaceful settlement of
disputes. Its jurisdiction was, indeed, even in the days of its
greatest power not universal. When in 1926 the Nicaraguan Government appealed to the League against Mexico, whose government was alleged to be assisting its political enemies, the United
States Government hurriedly sent a squadron of ships to Nicaragua "for the protection of American and foreign lives and prop-
erty"; and the League accepted this intimation that the maintenance of peace and order in Central America was not a matter in
which it need interest itself. The peculiar relations between Great
Britain and Egypt (which had been recognised as an independent
state in 1922) excluded Egypt from membership of the League,
and prevented differences of opinion between Great Britain and
Egypt from being treated as international disputes. Disputes between China and the Great Powers over the treaties which gave
foreigners special rights in China were not considered proper
matters for submission to the League. But notwithstanding these
exceptions, the sphere of action of the League was far-reaching;
and during these years disputes were referred to it from many
quarters of the world. By way of illustration, three of these disputes, all of them involving possible danger of war, will be described here.

The first arose under the treaty of peace with Turkey, which
provided that the frontier between Turkey and the mandated territory of Iraq should, in default of agreement between the British
and Turkish Governments, be determined by the Council of the
League. In the autumn of 1924 the Council, on which Turkey
(though not yet a member of the League) was represented for this
purpose, appointed a neutral boundary commission to recom-
mend a frontier line. The disputed area was the vilayet or district
of Mosul, which was inhabited by a mixed Kurdish, Turkish and
Arab population, and which had been in British occupation since
the armistice. While the boundary commission was at work, the
Kurds in Turkey, a hardy race of mountaineers, revolted against
the Turkish Government. The revolt was put down with traditional Turkish ferocity. Many Kurds fled into the Mosul area, and

there were serious clashes on the existing provisional frontier. The situation seemed so menacing that the Council of the League, early in 1925, sent out a second commission to report on these disturbances. The report was extremely unfavourable to Turkish methods of administration, and may have assisted the Council to fix a frontier which included practically the whole vilayet of Mosul in the mandated territory. During the last stage of the proceedings Turkey withdrew her representative from the Council, and went back on her previous undertaking to accept the Council's decision as final. The Permanent Court of International Justice, to which the matter was referred, gave its opinion that, under the Lausanne Treaty, the votes of the parties were not required to make the decision of the Council binding. After some hesitation, Turkey made the best of a bad job, and accepted the new frontier, which was confirmed by a treaty between Great Britain, Turkey and Iraq in June 1926.

The next dispute came from the Balkans. For many years after the war, the frontier between Greece and Bulgaria had been the scene of minor raids and disturbances, principally the work of Macedonian brigands. In October 1925 one of these incidents culminated in the murder of the commander of a Greek frontier post and one of his men. By way of reprisal, a Greek army marched into Bulgarian territory. The Bulgarian Government appealed to the League under Article 11 of the Covenant. The Council promptly met in Paris, exhorted the Greek Government to withdraw its troops, and requested the British, French and Italian Governments to send military officers to the spot to see what was happening. These measures exercised a deterrent effect on the Greek Government. The Greek forces retired from Bulgarian soil, and Greece was condemned to pay compensation to Bulgaria for the violation of her territory on a scale fixed by a League commission. Greece accepted the verdict. But there was some bitter comment on the different conception of justice which had prevailed two years before, when Greece suffered aggression, in precisely similar circumstances, at the hands of Italy.

The third dispute was one which had its roots in events already described. The Lithuanian Government, refusing to recognise the decision of the Allied Governments by which Poland had been left in possession of Vilna, severed relations with the Polish Government and proclaimed a "state of war" between the two countries. The frontier had ever since remained closed to traffic by road, rail or river; and this unnatural situation was aggravated by frequent frontier incidents and provocative pronouncements on both sides. In the autumn of 1927 Voldemaras, the stubborn little dictator of Lithuania, seized the occasion of an expulsion of some Lithuanians from Vilna to refer the whole matter to the League under Article 11 of the Covenant. On December 10th there was a memorable meeting of the Council at which the dictators of Lithuania and Poland (it was Pilsudski's only appearance at Geneva) confronted each other. This confrontation produced an agreed resolution of which the most notable feature was the declaration that "a state of war between two members of the League was incompatible with the spirit and the letter of the Covenant", and that Lithuania in consequence no longer considered herself in a state of war with Poland. The rest of the resolution was less promising. The "difference of opinion" about Vilna was not affected by it. The recommendation to the two governments to "enter into direct negotiations" on the other questions was not carried out, and there was no resumption of diplomatic or commercial relations. Nevertheless, the ventilation of this long-standing Polish-Lithuanian quarrel at Geneva did in fact lead to a lasting relaxation of tension, if not to a reconciliation, between the two countries; and it constituted a substantial success for the League.

The treatment of these three disputes by the League provokes some general reflexions. Both the Mosul and the Polish-Lithuanian disputes were disputes between states of very unequal strength. In both cases, the stronger state was not only in possession of the disputed territory, but had at any rate formal right on its side. In both these cases, the League performed the useful function of enabling the weaker state to climb down from an untenable position without loss of *amour-propre*. The Greco-Bulgarian dispute was between weak and equally matched states, neither of which had powerful friends on the Council. These factors made it particularly suitable for League action. It was easy for the Council to take an impartial decision and to secure its acceptance by the parties. No such fortunate conjunction of circumstances thereafter occurred in a dispute threatening an outbreak of hostilities; and this incident therefore remained the high-water mark of League achievement in preventing war.

The most noteworthy fact about all these successes of the League was, however, that they were achieved by methods of conciliation. In the two last cases, the procedure was governed by Articles 4 and 11 of the Covenant. Both parties to the dispute sat at the Council table, as provided by Article 4, with the full rights of members, including the right to vote; and this meant, under the unanimity rule, that no decision could be taken without the assent of the parties themselves. In the earlier stages of the Mosul dispute, exactly the same procedure was applied, though Turkey was not a member of the League; and though, in the final stage, this procedure was altered by the somewhat unexpected verdict of the Permanent Court based on the terms of the Lausanne Treaty, there was never any question of enforcing a decision. In all these cases it was recognised that the Council could proceed only by methods of persuasion. During this period of its greatest power and prestige, the League relied solely on its moral authority; for Article 11 of the Covenant conferred on it no other powers. Before 1932, no attempt was ever made to resort to the procedure of judgment and penalty provided in Articles 15 and 16.

Other Activities of the League

But though the preservation of peace was the League's most important and conspicuous function, no history of international relations after 1919 would be complete without some mention of what may be called the routine activities of the League, many of which became a recognised part of international life.

Some of these activities were political. The Mandates Commission, a body composed of eleven experts in colonial government, met twice a year at Geneva to receive annual reports from the Mandatory Powers on the territories administered by them, and to submit these to the Council with its comments and recommendations. The Council considered them and, if necessary, made recommendations on them, the Mandatory Power (whether a regular member of the Council or not) being represented on the Council for this purpose. A procedure of a different character had been devised for the execution of the minorities treaties. Petitions on behalf of minorities were submitted, together with the reply of the government against whom the complaint was made, to a committee of three members of the Council. The committee discussed the matter with the government (but not with the minority, which had no right to be heard), and generally concluded either by exonerating the government or by obtaining from it an undertaking to remedy the grievance complained of. If the committee failed to obtain satisfaction, it could refer the petition to the Council, on which the defendant government was, of course, represented. Thus both mandates and minorities procedures were based on the same principle as Article 11 of the Covenant, *i.e.* that decisions were reached by methods of persuasion and with the consent of the government concerned.

The League had other occasional political functions. It successfully administered the Saar territory, through a governing commission, from 1920 to 1935, and in January 1935 conducted the plebiscite there. No other territory was ever placed under direct League administration. But the League guaranteed the constitution of the Free City of Danzig, and was represented there by a High Commissioner, whose function was to arbitrate on disputes between the Free City and Poland. Both parties had the right of appeal to the Council against the High Commissioner's decisions. Before 1934, when the German-Polish agreement altered the position, no question appeared more frequently on the agenda of the Council than disputes between Poland and Danzig; and the League machine achieved a high degree of efficiency in dealing with these disputes.

The League provided a new and elaborate machinery for international co-operation in the economic sphere. Financial and economic committees composed of experts from various countries met annually at Geneva, and directed the work of the financial and economic sections of the League secretariat. The financial committee was responsible for the issue and supervision of the various League loans. A general financial conference was held at Brussels in 1920, and an economic conference at Geneva in 1927, the former being concerned with post-war financial reconstruction and the latter with the reduction of tariffs and other trade barriers.

The social and humanitarian work of the League was in part a co-ordination of sporadic international activities which had begun before the war, and in part broke fresh ground. The campaign against slavery was the most ancient of all these activities. A Slavery Convention was concluded at Geneva in 1925; and in 1932 the League decided to set up a Permanent Slavery Commission. Other League organisations dealt with the traffic in dangerous drugs, the traffic in women, the protection of children, the relief and settlement of refugees, and health and disease in their international aspects.

Finally, there were two international organisations which, though borne on the League budget, were administratively independent of the League: the International Labour Organisation and the Permanent Court of International Justice.

The International Labour Organisation, which had its seat at Geneva, was created by the peace treaties to provide for the improvement of labour conditions by international agreement. Its constitution was modelled on that of the League, its Annual Conference, Governing Body and Office corresponding respectively to the Assembly, Council and Secretariat. The International Labour Organisation was now composed of all the members of the League, together with the United States and Brazil. Each national delegation to the Annual Conference consisted of four delegates, two appointed by the government, one by employers' organisations and one by workers' organizations. A large number of international conventions dealing with various aspects of labour were concluded, but not all of them were generally ratified.

The Permanent Court of International Justice was established by the League under Article 14 of the Covenant for the purpose of deciding "any dispute of an international character which the parties thereto submit to it", and of giving "advisory opinions" on questions referred to it by the Council or the Assembly. It had a panel of fifteen judges appointed every nine years by the Council and the Assembly, and sat at the Hague. The statute of the Court contained a so-called "Optional Clause", signatories of which bound themselves to submit to it for decision any international dispute of a legal character between themselves and other League members; and about fifty states, including most of the Great Powers, signed this clause, some of them with certain reservations. The American Government twice made a move to adhere to the Permanent Court (on which there was always an American judge). But the proposal on each occasion fell through. Between 1922 and 1939, the Court pronounced more than fifty decisions and opinions. . . .

The League and Its Stance Against War

The years 1926 to 1929 were particularly fertile in schemes for strengthening security against war, each Assembly hailing the birth of some fresh proposal. . . .

A few days before the 1928 Assembly met, Paris was the scene of a striking and important ceremony: the signature of a pact for the renunciation of war, commonly known as the Pact of Paris or the Briand-Kellogg Pact. It is a little unfair that none of the immense public applause which greeted this event should have been bestowed on the League. For during the Assembly of 1927, which had already devoted so much thought to the problem of preventing war, the Polish Delegation had proposed a solemn declaration "that all wars of aggression are, and shall always be, prohibited"; and this declaration was unanimously adopted. . . .

This proposal was in due course accepted. On August 27th, 1928, the representatives of the six recognised Great Powers (the United States, Great Britain, France, Germany, Italy and Japan), the three other "Locarno Powers" (Belgium, Poland and Czechoslovakia) and the British Dominions and India, assembled in Paris to sign the pact. Every other independent state in the world was invited to accede to it.

The sense in which the signatories interpreted their undertaking to renounce war "as an instrument of national policy in their relations with one another" is explained in the correspondence between them which preceded its signature. The original authors of the pact had already declared that it did not ban war in self-defence. It was not an acceptance of the pacifist doctrine of non-resistance. Great Britain further made it clear that the right of self-defence included, in her case, the right to defend "certain regions of the world the welfare and integrity of which constitute a special and vital interest for our peace and safety". In the case of the United States, self-defence included any action required to prevent an infringement of the Monroe Doctrine. These explanations (for they were not treated as formal reservations) threw into relief the general character of the pact. It was regarded by many as a declaration of principle rather than a contractual obligation. Each state remained the sole judge of its own actions. No machinery for the interpretation or enforcement of the pact was set up or contemplated.

Imperfect though it was, the Pact of Paris was a considerable land-mark. It was the first political agreement in history of almost universal scope. The Argentine, Brazil, Bolivia and Salvador, aggrieved by the reassertion of the Monroe Doctrine, held aloof. But every other state, with insignificant exceptions, hastened to accede. The Soviet Union, after an initial moment of hesitation, was so enthusiastic that it proposed and concluded a special agreement with its neighbours to bring the Pact of Paris into force as between themselves in advance of the general ratification. No less than sixty-five states accepted the pact—a number exceeding by seven the current membership of the League of Nations. It is indeed probable that some states acceded rather from a desire to conform than from any belief in the utility of the pact. Flagrant violations of it were soon committed by Japan and Italy, the one thinly disguised as a police operation, the other, still more thinly, as a defensive war. But this did not destroy the significance of the fact that the nations, acting together, had been prepared to pronounce a ban on war as a normal and legitimate method of settling international disputes. The term "outlawry of war" used by the American sponsors of the Pact implied the existence of a universal, unwritten law against which war was declared to be an offence. No authority existed to punish violations of the law, or even to pronounce that the law had been violated. But the conception itself struck root in the political thought of the world.

CHRONOLOGY

1900

American troops sent to restore order during Boxer Rebellion in China; the International Ladies' Garment Workers Union is founded; Eastman Kodak introduces the one-dollar Brownie box camera; the first U.S. auto show is held; Sigmund Freud's *The Interpretation of Dreams* is published; Joseph Conrad's *Heart of Darkness* is published.

1901

President William McKinley is assassinated; forty-two-year-old Vice President Theodore Roosevelt becomes the youngest president in American history; Cuba becomes a U.S. protectorate; Booker T. Washington's autobiography *Up from Slavery* is published; President Roosevelt invites Booker T. Washington to dine at the White House, creating controversy; the largest trust of the period, U.S. Steel, is organized; the Socialist Party of America is founded; England's queen Victoria dies; Guglielmo Marconi sends the first wireless communication across the Atlantic.

1902

The U.S. government intervenes for the first time ever in a strike, the Great Anthracite Coal Strike; President Roosevelt prosecutes J.P. Morgan's Northern Securities Company for violating the Sherman Act; Willis Carris invents the air conditioner.

1903

The Ford Motor Company is established; Orville and Wilbur Wright achieve the first controlled, powered flight in an airplane; the first national wildlife refuge, Pelican Island, Florida, is named; W.E.B. Du Bois's *The Souls of Black Folk* is published; Jack London's *The Call of the Wild* is published; the American League's Boston Red Sox baseball team beats the National League's Pittsburgh team in the first World Series; *The Great Train Robbery*, the first narrative film ever made, is released and becomes a box-office hit; Panama splits from Colombia and grants the United States the right to build the Panama Canal.

1904

Theodore Roosevelt is elected to his second term as president of the United States; the government announces the Roosevelt Corollary to the Monroe Doctrine; the Supreme Court dissolves the Northern Securities Company; Russia and Japan go to war; the World's Fair—the Louisiana Purchase Exposition—opens in St. Louis; Anton Chekhov writes *The Cherry Orchard.*

1905

The Industrial Workers of the World (IWW) is founded in Chicago; Albert Einstein's special theory of relativity is published.

1906

An earthquake and fire levels two-thirds of the city of San Francisco; a hurricane strikes Galveston, Texas, resulting in the worst recorded natural disaster in North American history; Upton Sinclair's *The Jungle* is published; construction of the Panama Canal gets under way; U.S. troops occupy Cuba to put down a revolt; Theodore Roosevelt wins the Nobel Prize for peace for his mediation of the Russo-Japanese War.

1907

Robert Peary reaches the North Pole; President Roosevelt bars Japanese immigration to the United States; more than 360 miners are killed in an explosion in Monograph, West Virginia, the nation's worst mining disaster to that time; Pablo Picasso paints *Les Demoiselles d'Avignon.*

1908

William Howard Taft is elected president of the United States; Henry Ford introduces the Model T; Jack Johnson becomes the first African American heavyweight boxing champion.

1909

The National Association for the Advancement of Colored People (NAACP) is founded; Matthew Henson and Robert Peary reach the North Pole.

1910

President Taft initiates "dollar diplomacy" in Nicaragua; architect Frank Lloyd Wright completes Robie House in Chicago; the Mann-Elkins Railroad Act hands increased power to the Interstate Commerce Commission to regulate certain industries; the first issue of black activist W.E.B. Du Bois's *The Crisis* appears; Eugene Ely flies the first aircraft from the deck of a ship, bringing air power and sea power together for the first time.

1911

Norwegian explorer Roald Amundsen reaches the South Pole; fire breaks out in the Triangle Shirtwaist Company of New York, killing 146 workers. The incident leads to a government investigation of shoddy factory conditions; the Supreme Court breaks up the Standard Oil Company of New Jersey because of monopolistic practices; pioneer aviator Cal Rodgers flies coast to coast; the Mexican Revolution takes place; Ernest Rutherford discovers the structure of the atom.

1912

New Mexico becomes the forty-seventh state; Arizona becomes the forty-eighth state; more than fifteen hundred passengers drown in the Atlantic after the ocean liner *Titanic* hits an iceberg and sinks; worker's rights activist Mother Jones leads a strike in West Virginia; the federal government extends the eight-hour workday to all federal employees; Jim Thorpe wins two Olympic gold medals but is subsequently stripped of them when it is revealed that he once played sports as a professional; Woodrow Wilson is elected president; the Balkan Wars take place.

1913

Suffragettes march in Washington, D.C., to demand the right to vote for women; the Seventeenth Amendment to the Constitution takes effect, providing for the direct election of U.S. senators; Igor Stravinsky composes *The Rite of Spring*; Henry Ford creates the moving assembly line.

1914

Henry Ford stuns the automotive world by announcing that he will pay his laborers the then-unheard-of sum of five dollars per

day; the archduke of Austria-Hungary is assassinated; World War
I begins; the Panama Canal opens and thereby shortens the travel
time and distance from the Atlantic to the Pacific Ocean.

1915

In New York, Alexander Graham Bell, inventor of the telephone,
conducts the first transcontinental telephone conversation when
he talks to his assistant, Thomas A. Watson, in San Francisco;
D.W. Griffith's motion picture *The Birth of a Nation* opens; over
one hundred Americans drown when a German submarine sinks
the passenger ship *Lusitania* in the Atlantic Ocean; this incident
brought the neutral United States to the brink of war with Germany; Charlie Chaplin stars in *The Tramp*; Turks slaughter up to
2 million Armenians; Einstein publishes the general theory of
relativity.

1916

Francisco "Pancho" Villa, rebel Mexican leader, leads a raid into
New Mexico that results in the death of seventeen Americans; in
response to the Villa raid, President Woodrow Wilson sends an
American military force into Mexico led by General John J. Pershing; the troops pursue Villa in Mexico until the following January; Woodrow Wilson is reelected president; Jeannette Rankin
serves as the first woman in Congress.

1917

Three American ships are sunk in the Atlantic Ocean by German
submarines; the United States declares war on Germany when
the European nation refuses to stop its unrestricted submarine
warfare in the Atlantic Ocean; Congress passes the Espionage
Act, which makes it a crime for an American citizen to assist an
enemy nation in any way; the Communist Bolshevik Party seizes
control in Russia and removes the nation from the war.

1918

Woodrow Wilson delivers his "Fourteen Points" speech to Congress, in which he proposes his plan for world peace; an influenza
epidemic breaks out in Europe and spreads to the United States;
over half a million Americans die from the disease worldwide;
World War I ends when Germany agrees to cease hostilities.

1919

Peace talks open in Paris; the Eighteenth Amendment to the Constitution, banning the manufacture and sale of alcohol, is ratified; Prohibition goes into effect the next year; Treaty of Versailles is signed in France, officially ending World War I; massive strike occurs against U.S. Steel and other companies that use the twelve-hour workday; military force is finally required to break the strike; the Volstead Act, which hands power to the police to enforce Prohibition, is passed; when it takes effect on January 16, 1920, Prohibition becomes the law of the land; the Black Sox scandal tarnishes baseball's image when members of the Chicago White Sox accept money to lose ball games; Englishmen John Alcock and Arthur Whitten-Brown fly nonstop across the Atlantic; the Versailles Treaty is signed; Mahatma Gandhi begins a nonviolent resistance movement in India.

FOR FURTHER RESEARCH

The American Heritage History of Flight. New York: Simon and Schuster, 1962.

Pierre Averous, *The Atom.* New York: Barron's, 1985.

Bruno Bettelheim, *Freud and Man's Soul.* New York: Knopf, 1983.

William Bloodworth Jr., *Upton Sinclair.* Boston: Twayne, 1977.

Maurice Bruce, *The Shaping of the Modern World.* New York: Random House, 1958.

E.H. Carr, *The Russian Revolution.* New York: Free, 1979.

Don Congdon, ed., *Combat: World War I.* New York: Dell, 1964.

Peter Cowie, ed., *A Concise History of the Cinema.* Vol. 1. London: Zwemmer, 1971.

Richard Crabb, *Birth of a Giant.* Philadelphia: Chilton, 1969.

C.H. Dodd and Mary Sales, *Israel and the Arab World.* New York: Barnes and Noble, 1970.

Reuben Fine, *Freud: A Critical Re-Evaluation of His Theories.* New York: McKay, 1962.

Simha Flapan, *Zionism and the Palestinians.* New York: Croom Helm, 1979.

Peter Gay, *Freud.* New York: Norton, 1988.

Mary Mathews Gedo, *Picasso: Art as Autobiography.* Chicago: University of Chicago Press, 1980.

Deborah Gerner, *One Land, Two Peoples.* Boulder, CO: Westview, 1991.

Hamlyn History of the Movies. London: Hamlyn, 1975.

Fred Howard, *Wilbur and Orville.* New York: Knopf, 1988.

W.P. Jolly, *Marconi.* New York: Stein and Day, 1972.

T.E. Lawrence, *Seven Pillars of Wisdom.* New York: Doubleday, 1935.

Donald Lopez, *Aviation.* New York: Macmillan, 1995.

Walter Lord, *A Night to Remember.* New York: Holt, 1955.

Don Lynch, *"Titanic": An Illustrated History.* New York: Hyperion, 1992.

Ian Macdonald, *1915.* New York: Holt, 1993.

Robert K. Massie, *Dreadnought.* New York: Ballantine, 1991.

Mertin Middlebrook, *First Day on the Somme.* New York: Norton, 1972.

Edmund Morris, *The Rise of Theodore Roosevelt.* New York: Coward, McCann & Geoghegan, 1979.

————, *Theodore Rex.* New York: Random House, 2001.

Roger Pethybridge, *Witnesses to the Russian Revolution.* New York: Citadel, 1967.

D.J. Raine, *Albert Einstein and Relativity.* New York: Crane, 1975.

Quentin Reynolds, *They Fought for the Sky.* New York: Holt, 1957.

John Richardson, *A Life of Picasso.* New York: Random House, 1996.

Sarah R. Riedman, *Men and Women Behind the Atom.* London: Abelard-Schuman, 1958.

John Severance, *Einstein.* New York: Clarion, 1999.

Kip Thorne, *Black Holes and Time Warps.* New York: Norton, 1994.

Barbara Tuchman, *The Proud Tower.* New York: Macmillan, 1966.

Richard M. Watt, *The Kings Depart.* New York: Clarion, 1968.

Jeremy Wilson, *Lawrence of Arabia.* New York: Atheneum, 1990.

Leon Wolff, *In Flanders Fields.* New York: Ballantine, 1958.

INDEX